Anxiety in Relationship

The Ultimate Toolkit to Relieve from Anxiety, Stress, Shyness, Depression and Phobias to Stop Worrying About Relationships.

A.P. COLLINS

Introduction

Whether you or your partner, are suffering from anxiety, you have already taken the first major step on the path to self-improvement by purchasing *Anxiety in Relationship: The Ultimate Toolkit for Relief from Anxiety, Stress, Shyness, Depression, Phobias and for Self-Development to Stop Worrying about Panic Attacks.*

The purpose of this book is to put you on the right track and help you understand every aspect of anxiety and how it's influencing your life. As well understand each form of anxiety so that you can make the right changes and decision in order to fight it. This affliction affects a great deal of people, and it can also affect your relationship. This book will aide you on your journey of self-development and will help you find the relief you seek.

What you will Learn

You begin by learning all you need to know about anxiety and how it affects your life and relationships. You will discover each type of anxiety disorder and learn what makes them tick. Gaining an understanding of your suffering is the first step in putting your life back on track.

Next, we continue the discussion by placing our focus on anxiety-driven relationships. You will learn how your relationship can be affected due to your anxiety and what kind of behaviors it can cause. Often relationships are damaged because there is no understanding within the relationship, and everyone is acting based on their anxiety-driven feelings.

Once you gain a full understanding of anxiety, we will dive deeper into the subject. We will discuss the negative beliefs you formed in early life, that can affect your current relationship. Then continue the discussion by

6

analyzing the most common disorders that cause anxiety, such as obsessive-compulsive relationship disorder, abandonment anxiety disorder, and philophobia.

Finally, you will learn how to improve your relationship by enhancing your communication skills, recognizing your mistakes, taking responsibility, offering support, and much more. Relationships often suffer needlessly due to a lack of understanding caused by anxiety-driven behaviors. You will also learn various techniques such as mindful breathing and visualization, to combat your anxiety more effectively.

With that said, congratulations on taking the first step on your journey by recognizing that you need a little help. Now, let's start addressing your anxiety problems!

Chapter 1: Understanding Anxiety

Everyone experiences anxiety in one form or another during their lifetime. Just take a walk in the park, and most people you walk by have either experienced an anxiety episode in the past or are currently suffering from one. At least half of these people struggle with sleeping problems, restlessness, shortness of breath, overactive mind, sweaty palms, and so on. On top of that, many don't ever seek treatment for this average occurrence. The rate of anxiety disorders is climbing and shows no signs of stopping. Modern technology has exposed us to images of natural disasters, terrorism, crimes, war, financial collapse, and this has led to an increase in anxiety. Experiencing minor anxiety is a normal biological response that plays a vital role in life. Without it we could not respond correctly to outliers putting our lives at risk. However, too much can bring chaos into our homes, affect work, bars a full and happy life, and it can even tear relationships apart.

While everyone is exposed to some form of anxiety, watching someone you love suffering will greatly impact your life and significantly reduce its quality. It can lead to deeper issues, and their anxiety will have a more substantial impact on you. Feeling sympathy and trying to alleviate the pain, is normal but it's common to develop feelings of frustration, sadness, resentment, and even anger with this person. Fixing a relationship can sometimes feel like a burden, and that may develop into its own form of anxiety. Even if you were always aware of your partner's anguish, it can wear you down. Keep in mind that this is just one example scenario that can ruin a relationship, and isn't even about you, but the other person.

Relationship anxiety and anxiety, in general, involve complex issues that stem from a variety of sources. That is why, in this chapter, we are going to focus on understanding relationship anxiety. You need to know what it is, how it affects you and your partner, and how it manifests itself. You need to understand the problem so that you can combat it at its source instead of just treating the symptoms that will eventually erode your relationship.

What is Anxiety?

Anxiety can be broken down into feelings of worry, fear, and uneasiness, and it is a mental disorder that is most commonly encountered. The number of people suffering from anxiety has been steadily growing, so if you are suffering, you shouldn't blame or hate yourself because you are far from being alone.

The causes of anxiety are incredibly diverse and can't be pinpointed down to one specific occurrence. Keep in mind that humans are hardwired to experience anxiety because it is crucial to our survival. Small doses of anxiety can be beneficial as it increases your level of focus and alertness; however, the adverse effects usually outweigh the positive ones. Certain people are more susceptible to its effects, but most research has trouble finding an explanation for this.

Everyone reacts differently to anxiety and the cause can be rooted in genetics, personal trauma, self-esteem, stress exposure, and other psychological conditions. The result of this affliction is in fact a highly subjective experience. One person's light feeling of stress can be someone else's full-blown panic attack. This is one of the reasons why we think of anxiety as an emotion, as it manifests itself differently depending on the person, and so does the intensity. Mild anxiety can make you more productive, help you stick to your deadlines, and pay your bills on time. Higher levels can lead you down a dark path filled with psychological, or physical problems. These problems are why it's essential to be able to tell the difference between everyday anxiety that will pass, and anxiety attacks that need to be diagnosed. One main characteristic that sets these two forms of anxiety apart is whether you still experience the feeling of stress when the tense situation has passed. Now, let's examine the most common forms of anxiety and symptoms.

Common Symptoms

As mentioned above, everyone experiences anxiety as it involves an array of symptoms. Some people struggle with their day to day life without knowing it's due to an undiagnosed anxiety disorder. This is why you should be familiar with symptoms that manifest themselves as behavioral, physical or emotional issues. Some may experience them all at once, while others discover that their anxiety is rooted in one specific area. While anxiety is perceived entirely at an individual level, there are also recognizable patterns. Here are some of the common signs of anxiety:

1. **Behavioral Signs**: The way you, or your partner, behave when being faced with anxiety can give you the feedback you need in order to gain a better insight into the internal struggle. Anxiety triggers the same or similar behavioral symptoms in many people. For instance, you might avoid certain events such as parties, or areas that involve minor social interaction such as an elevator. You might stay away from anxiety-inducing situations that make you uncomfortable, like crowded restaurants and movie theaters. Another sign is compulsive behavior such as repeatedly washing your hands or obsessing over how many times you have locked the door. Many who suffer from anxiety will also limit what kind of everyday activities they perform. Even when in a loving relationship, a partner can feel reluctant from engaging in outdoor couple's activities and giving in to this type of feeling can make things worse. Finally, one of the worst and most destructive behavior signs is giving into extensive alcohol or drugs consumption.

2. **Physical Signs**: Keep in mind that most physical symptoms are normal reactions and responses that don't necessarily prove that

you are suffering from an anxiety disorder. Some of these signs involve increased sweating, shaking, feeling restless, having issues sleeping even when feeling tired, nausea, dizziness, stomach irritation, and more. Other physical symptoms include a stronger reaction when someone surprises you or approaches you from behind without letting you know that they are there. All of these reactions are self-defense mechanisms, and you shouldn't conclude from these experiences alone. Keep in mind it's the severity of the response that determines the level of anxiety. Its effects and duration determine whether or not you are suffering from a disorder, and not just having a normal reaction to stress or fear.

3. **Emotional Signs**: We discussed earlier that anxiety is, in fact, an emotion, and therefore, it can trigger a wide variety of feelings when dealing with it. You or your partner might experience anxiety in the form of fear, panic, pressure, stress, or a feeling of being overwhelmed, among many others. Another emotional signs dread, or when you feel that something isn't quite right, but you can pinpoint what causes that emotion.

While you are aware of the most common symptoms, you also need to understand that not all of these behaviors and emotions necessarily relate to an anxiety disorder. It's vital for you, as well as your partner, to be able to make the distinction between daily anxiety and real disorders.

There's a thin line between a serious health condition and feelings of anxiety. An undiagnosed condition can cause undue stress on relationships. And this can cause an afflicted person to minimize severe problems and explode or add pressure on a partner by overestimating mild anxiousness. The main reason this distinction even exists is because it merely depends on how people express their symptoms and how they feel their life is affected.

An example that exists in many relationships is work-related stress. Let's say you have an important meeting or work presentation that you've been preparing for weeks but are still having difficulty. This stress can cause a great deal of pressure, making you feel anxious, irritable or cause you to lose sleep. It could be a day to day anxiety or signs of a deeper problem, namely an anxiety disorder. It all depends on how strong the symptoms manifest themselves and whether you still experience them after the presentation is over. In the case of everyday anxiety, your feelings of anxiety would pass almost immediately once the stressful situation is over. However, if you find you are still feeling them, or you experience anxiety about another situation, you might be dealing with a disorder.

Imagine anxiety as an early alarm system that's triggered to warn you about potential danger. It's a good thing to have and keeps you alert. The problem for people suffering from anxiety disorders is the slightest mishap can trigger this alarm, therefore making life a lot more stressful than it should be. This issue is how you can find yourself in a constant state of anxiety.

The number of people suffering from this affliction is tremendous, and you are not alone, as anxiety and its disorders are extremely common. Luckily, these afflictions are easily treatable. So why are so many people suffering, you may ask? Because so many of them don't solicit help or find a suitable mental health professional to talk through the critical issues. If you haven't been diagnosed and feel afflicted you should never self-diagnose or diagnose your significant other. Use the knowledge from this book to educate yourselves and understand how anxiety works to find a possible solution. Next, let's take a look at the most common types of anxiety disorders.

Anxiety Disorders

Six main types of anxiety have a significant impact on your life, as well as your relationship:

1. Generalized Anxiety Disorder

2. Obsessive-Compulsive Disorder

3. Post-Traumatic Stress Disorder

4. Social Anxiety Disorder (also known as Social Phobia)

5. Panic Disorder

6. Various Phobias

Every single disorder on this list needs to be diagnosed by a professional by following specific criteria. However, keep in mind that while various unique characteristics define each disorder, some of them will overlap. It is fairly common to be diagnosed with multiple disorders. It is relatively common for a multiple disorder diagnosis, so we will explore a real scenario to gain a better understanding of what makes each one special.

Generalized Anxiety Disorder

Imagine a person called John, he is the owner of a start-up company. As a newly established entrepreneur, he feels that he is always stressed out, even over the most trivial things. Thoughts such as *Will the business manage to generate enough profit to stay afloat? Will he and his partner, Jane, manage to earn enough to afford college for their children? Is he feeling constantly tired simply because of work, or is he sick? What if his taxes will be audited and something goes wrong? How will he and Jane manage if something goes wrong and the house requires a serious repair?* At this point, John understands that most of his fears are unfounded and unlikely to ever turn into reality. Despite this fact, he still can't manage to calm down and clear his mind. His partner, Jane, tries to help by assuring him that everything will be fine, but she is unable to comfort him.

John is a classic case of generalized anxiety disorder. Those who are suffering from this psychological ailment often live out their lives always worried about something, even when there is no real basis for that worry. People like John always expect some disaster to occur. Whether it involves finances, health, or relationships, however, it never manifests itself outside of their thoughts. Generalized anxiety causes people to struggle with letting go of excessive worries, even if they are aware are mostly a figment of their imagination. Other disorder such as an eating disorder, depression, or excessive drug use can characterize it.

Generalized anxiety disorder doesn't always manifest itself as a destructive force and builds up gradually. People suffering from a slight version of this disorder don't usually have problems building a career, a relationship, or handling their responsibilities. On the other hand, those suffering from a severe case of generalized anxiety will struggle to fulfill the most basic tasks. However, keep in mind that avoiding various situations such as going out on a date, avoiding elevator rides, or driving isn't symptoms of this disorder. They are simple phobias.

Obsessive-Compulsive Disorder

Now imagine Joan, a 38-year-old mother who has two children. She always seems to find herself with the uncontrollable urge to wash her hands multiple times after performing activities. If Joan takes a walk in the park or exposes her hands to something considered dirty, she needs to scrub them precisely 12 times to feel clean. The repetition is a comfort until she touches something else, and she will need to start over. The constant washing leads to physical problems such as irritated skin and bleeding hands. Even with all of the pain, she cannot stop. Her significant other is starting to worry about Joan as she doesn't want to stop and listen to her concerns.

This example is a perfect case of obsessive-compulsive disorder, as Joan is incapable of controlling her desire to wash her hands after touching something or someone. As the name suggests, people like Joan have obsessions, in the form of thoughts or beliefs, they feel forced to perform as a particular ritual to alleviate the source of stress. These compulsive rites are supposed to offer relief, even if they don't invoke pleasure. People suffering from OCD do this as if there's no other option to reduce their levels of anxiety induced by the obsession

For instance, someone who follows the same morning routine out of the fear of forgetting something or being late for work doesn't suffer from this anxiety disorder. The key difference between this example and Joan's situation that a compulsive obsession doesn't drive the habit. Those diagnosed with OCD cannot properly function each day if they do not perform a specific ritual. These habits control their lives, while those without OCD can adapt to a situation no matter how stubborn they are.

This extreme hand sanitizing example, as well as any other germ fear, is just one form of obsessive-compulsive disorder. Some people may be obsessed with their home security, for instance, and therefore invest a great deal into locks and then perform a safety check on all of the doors and windows. Other people may find relief for their anxiety by merely touching certain objects in a special pattern, or by counting up to a certain number. Another common form of OCD is experiencing the irresistible need for achieving perfect symmetry. Establishing the "perfect" order can become a lifetime challenge that will prevent some people from being able to function regularly inside an office environment or even at home.

OCD can sometimes accompany other anxiety disorders, depression, as well as eating disorders. Often people dive into heavy drug use as well because they find that the substances reduce the amount of anxiety they experience.

Post-Traumatic Stress Disorder

Imagine Mark, a young 23-year-old man who has served the military for five years and has completed two tours of active duty in war zones. Now that he has completed his last deployment, he decided to leave the military and settle down together with his fiancé, Lisa. However, he's been experiencing severe difficulties trying to readapt to civilian life and building a new home. He has trouble sleeping and when he does finally fall asleep, he has nightmares about screaming and dying people. When he's awake and going on with his day, he's often startled by loud, unexpected sounds. Whenever Lisa tries to surprise him from behind, Mark freaks out. He also experiences flashbacks on occasion, which forces him to relive the combat anxiety as he starts to remember the smell and taste of it all. All of these events are beginning to tear the relationship apart as Mark starts losing his grip on reality. Lisa becomes afraid of him as he often goes into outbursts of rage or has overreactions towards safety as if he still fighting a war.

This entire scenario is a typical example of post-traumatic stress disorder or PTSD. You may know from the media has been covering it extensively due to a large number of combat veterans experiencing it. However, this disorder doesn't just develop because of traumatic combat experience. The root of it can stem from any traumatic experience, such as the victim of robbery, assault, or even early childhood bullying. The trigger for this anxiety disorder can be related to a traumatic event that happened to you directly, or that you witnessed happening to someone you care deeply about.

As you can probably tell from the story, the most common PTSD symptoms involve aggressive behavior, obsessing over safety, lashing out violently towards others, and being easily startled. The lack of emotions, intimacy issues and unapproachable behavior make it difficult to go through the day. People who have PTSD relive their awful memories whether they are awake or asleep, and they often show up in the form of flashbacks. The flashback is triggered by a particular sound or smell associated with the traumatic event, however you won't be able to tell it isn't reality. Images, smells, sounds and even emotions can rush over you and take you back to that traumatic experience that started it all. Even during sleep, there is often no relief as dreams are haunted by these thoughts.

Some of the symptoms can occur over a brief period, as not everyone develops PTSD directly after a tragedy. To be diagnosed, the symptoms would be present for around four weeks, and even the duration of the disorder varies from person to person. It's not always a permanent form of anxiety. Some people manage to overcome the trauma after a short amount of time, while others need to learn how to live with it. Self-destructive behavior such as drug or alcohol abuse is also common among people living with PTSD as they try to use anything to dull the traumatic memories.

Panic Disorder

Thomas is a college student about to graduate, and he's getting ready to take his final exams. Just like any other student, he's feeling anxious as these exams are important and will determine his future. However, during one seemingly ordinary day, while studying a challenging subject, he starts to feel strange. He is having difficulty breathing, experiencing chest pains and he's sweating profusely. The pain only lasted a few minutes but was sharp, and with no previous health problems, it made him nervous. Thomas didn't seek help at first, but his overly concerned girlfriend convinces him to go to the emergency room for tests. He reluctantly yields to her requests and heads to urgent care to get tested. The tests came out negative however, and this only increased both of their concerns that something more serious might be happening. *What if this happens again while Thomas is driving and he ends up causing an accident and taking someone's life?*

This situation is scary for anyone as it can have dire secondary effects, on innocent bystanders in the wrong place at the wrong time. What Thomas experienced was a panic attack, and it occurred when he was sitting at his desk, studying for finals. A panic attack can happen at any time without warning before. It manifests suddenly, accompanied by an extreme sensation of fear and dread, together with intense sweating, dizziness, chest pain, and nausea. Because of the sheer number of physical symptoms, some people go into a deeper state of panic once the episode is over. They think they're about to pass out or have a fatal heart attack. While panic attacks may indeed resemble heart attacks due to the common symptoms, you will usually survive, however if one were to occur while driving or working with power tools it can endanger your life. Suffering from a panic attack while driving or working with dangerous tools can endanger your life Keep in mind that panic attacks are so unpredictable that they can occur even during sleep. This is why they are mistaken for heart attacks as they can wake a person out of a calm sleep with painful symptoms.

While a panic attack usually doesn't last for more than a few minutes, it can lead to long-lasting or even permanent symptoms. Why? Because those who undergo such a frightening experience end up living with the fear of it happening again. This is enough for most people to develop other anxiety disorders and even have new panic attacks as a result of this fear.

Panic attacks, unlike certain anxiety disorders, can lead to a closed-off life because fear keeps people from their daily routine. Asking themselves: "What if I have a panic attack while on my way to work and I end up killing someone?" or "What if it happens when I'm working with heavy machinery and I hurt one of my coworkers?". These haunting questions turn a panic attack into a deep feeling of anxiety which can then lead to conditions such as agoraphobia. Phobias can develop easily as well. Naturally, in such cases where life becomes so restricted, the situation can place a lot of strain on even the most solid relationship. Living with a person who is too afraid to leave the house, go to work, or perform any physical task can be a problematic and life-altering choice for anyone.

Social Anxiety Disorder

Imagine Emma, a lead software developer working at a large tech company. She's been growing her career in that business for over ten years but lives under the constant fear that she might be fired. Despite the fact that her peer reviews are positive, she turns in excellent work, and she is a massive asset to her team, Emma will tense up whenever someone comments on her work or offers criticism. Even if the comment is coming from her teammate and it isn't critical, she struggles, thinking her work isn't good enough. Even if the comment is coming from her teammate and it isn't critical, she struggles, thinking her work isn't good enough. On top of this reaction, Emma avoids banter with her colleagues, preferring to work through the day without interaction. Emma regularly declines invitations to social events because she's afraid that her colleagues won't like her. She firmly believes that if she quits, or is fired, she will never find another job because her skills aren't good enough. The thoughts and concerns have seeped into her marriage, as her husband is always trying to help. Nothing has improved, and now their relationship is suffering because he ignores her when she talks about work.

This example is a clear case of social anxiety disorder, as someone like Emma can experience a great deal of stress whenever she is in the same room with other people. These people often obsess over social encounter days before they happen. In Emma's case, she is self-conscious about her performance at work, as well as the opinion of her colleagues. This fear is impacting her life and intimate relationships.

In many similar cases, people are rarely successful in school or work because of the difficulty they find in building relationships, as well as the constant self-doubt. If you think you are not good enough to be employed, you could end up in a position you hate, wasting life because of your socially overwhelmed brain. Social anxiety is powerful and can control many aspects of your life. A small amount of fear when giving a speech is normal, but the anxiety is overwhelming and causes you to quit, then it's a problem that needs attention.

Keep in mind that social anxiety disorder can manifest itself either in a very specific and sometimes limited fashion, such as encounters with your boss or participating in a group activity. For instance, some people will stop performing a task if someone is looking over their shoulder out of fear of their work being judged and criticized. However, anxiety can also manifest itself in a broader sense, such as an activity involving people that aren't your immediate relatives or close friends. With this in mind, here are several situations that cause paralyzing fear in people suffering from this disorder:

1. Performing any activity in front of others. For example, writing while someone is overlooking.

2. Holding a casual conversation with a coworker or a stranger.

3. Joining any group activity, debate, or discussion. This includes asking a question in front of the group.

4. Most social gatherings and events.

5. Coming into contact with new people.

6. Interacting with anyone who has authoritative power. A student may experience social anxiety when faced with asking the teacher a question. The same thing can happen when facing a supervisor or manager at work.

7. Using public facilities.

8. Making unplanned phone calls, especially to a stranger.

People who suffer from social anxiety disorder are nearly always aware of their fears and doubts. They understand that they have an exaggerated view of all these concerns and situations we listed above. The difference is they don't feel like they have any power or control over their thoughts and beliefs. This isn't the same thing as being shy. People with social phobia have a hard time getting over their anxiety when they find themselves in the middle of a triggering situation. While people who are shy, or mildly anxious, lose the fear almost immediately when the situation is over. An example of mild anxiety in this situation might be a student dreading a presentation in class, but when the time comes and he starts talking about it, the feeling is gone. People with extreme social anxiety will experience that anxiety during the entire presentation. In some cases, they will obsess over their behavior for days, examining their performance. They may even attempt to get inside the minds of classmates who were present to find out their opinions.

Social anxiety can be impairing and extremely destructive. As a result, establishing a relationship can be hard, but maintaining it can be even more challenging. A large number of people with this disorder also try to self-medicate with various substances, thinking it helps them calm down. Drug use in this scenario usually leads to more problems down the road and even a full-blown dependence on the substance.

Phobias

Imagine Sam, a hard working sales executive at a financial firm. His duties require him to work over twelve hours a day, making a large number of phone calls and regularly traveling to discuss deals with clients. Despite long hours and exhaustion he convinces himself, as well as others, that he loves the active pace and the challenges that come with his position. However, he sometimes has to take long flights to reach certain clients, and during these flights, he experiences a rapid heart rate, excessive sweating and troubling thoughts. To control this situation, Sam stops taking long-distance clients so he can avoid flying. This leads to a problem as his partner, Jen, loves to travel. Sam comes up with excuse after excuse to avoid getting on a plane, and they eventually stop taking most trips together. Jen becomes extremely frustrated by this over time, and starts questioning their relationship. Loneliness and resentment grow between them without either person realizing.

As you might be able to tell Sam started suffering from a phobia, which is an irrational fear of something that wouldn't typically give him any cause for concern. A lot of people experience these phobias, and they are aware of them in most cases; however, they feel they have no control over their reaction. Even the thought of what scares them is enough to trigger a feeling of anxiety, or in more extreme cases, a panic attack.

Here are some examples of common irrational fears: fear of flying, closed spaces, elevators, heights, needles, blood, insects, animals, storms, etc. The even more fascinating aspect of any phobia is their ability to be even more specific. Take the fear of heights, for example. Someone may manage to climb a mountain with no problems and look below at the stunning landscape, even if they're afraid of heights. At the same time, this person experiences an anxiety attack when going to the fourth floor of an apartment building.

Phobias can restrict someone's quality of life and even damage relationships in multiple ways. For instance, let's say that someone arranges a date at a restaurant located across a bridge, and the only way to get to it is by crossing the bridge. If this person has an intense fear of bridges, that date is likely to be canceled or rescheduled provided the other person understands the situation. On the other hand, someone with a needle phobia will avoid getting checked at the hospital under any circumstance. Another person with an aversion towards cats will panic at the sight of one, making it impossible for him to live with someone who has a pet cat.

A lot of these irrational fears usually develop during childhood, but they can also appear at any time during someone's lifetime. Without treatment, life can become unbearable as every aspect of it will eventually be damaged. However, certain phobias won't always become a problem in a relationship. For instance, let's say you have an irrational fear of monkeys, but because they are region specific, the chances of you encountering one in daily life is zero. This kind of fear will allow you to live a normal life.

Chapter 2: Anxiety in Relationships

Nearly every facet of a relationship is affected by anxiety, no matter what type. When someone enters into a relationship, there are relatively simple expectations that go along with it. First and foremost, you assume the other person can fulfill the role of a partner. Being a partner involves a solid ability to communicate openly, offer companionship, contribute financially, hold onto a stable job, and eventually raise a family.

Over the years, a variety of studies on people suffering from different forms of anxiety and disorders help us understand. They started realizing their condition was affecting their relationships with parents, significant other, spouse, or coworkers. Many have admitted that anxiety disorders such as generalized anxiety disorder have played a massive role in damaging the relationship. Fortunately, many of these disorders are now treatable. When anxiety is out of the picture or under proper control, a relationship with loved ones once again could grow.

In this chapter, we are going to discuss anxiety's connection to relationships and how it can affect them. You will find various examples and exercises at the end of each section to help you identify whether your relationship is being affected by a form of anxiety.

Relationship Communication

As you should know, communication is particularly important when it comes to romantic relationships. Being able to discuss all issues freely, make plans, and set goals for the future are all vital for a successful relationship. Otherwise, how could two partners handle their responsibilities, challenges, and expectations?

However, what happens if one of you is suffering from anxiety? Any of the disorders we discussed earlier can have a severe impact on your ability to maintain a healthy way to communicate in your relationship. Of course, it depends on how severe the anxiety is. However, no matter its level of development, a personal connection will be in some way affected. You or your partner might encounter difficulties in reacting in a healthy way when either of you expresses an opinion or an emotion. For instance, it is common to misread someone's intent or misinterpret the meaning of individual conversations. Anxiety works in many ways as a filter, and when it clouds your vision, you might act in a way that will eventually damage your relationship. Any joke, comment, or harmless critique can lead to an overreaction that will put a strain on any couple, even more than the anxiety itself.

If you find yourself in such a situation you should take a break and see what warranted such a negative reaction, or outburst. Your partner may be suffering from a form of anxiety, and they are overwhelmed by the strain. On the other side, if you are the one with this problem, you need to acknowledge what's wrong and express it. If not, your partner will think you're cruel or aggressive for no reason, or that they are the problem.

Relationship Communication Anxiety

Anxiety has a severe emotional effect on people, and the partner is always affected in some way as a result of seeing his or her significant other suffering and going through the whole life crippling experience. And many cases in which the one suffering from anxiety will suppress any emotion or feeling. Emotions carry a great deal of power, and some people find it too challenging to face them. Those who are afraid to express themselves emotionally have likely lived in a household where the behavior was discouraged.

The act of suppressing emotions is a sign that the person is trying to hold onto a semblance of control. If you find yourself behaving this way, it might be because you are scared at the thought of losing that control and allowing the locked-up feelings to overwhelm you. Naturally, the biggest issue here is when it comes to negative emotions as they have such a substantial impact on a person's life. You might think that if you let it all out, you will change your partner's feelings. And whatever good opinions and thoughts he or she has about you will be gone, cause damage to the relationship. However, while you may think of this as a solution, it leads to even more problems. Acting this way will increase the amount of anxiety you experience. You will find less and less peace of mind, until one day when it will all come out in a wild burst. It's difficult to suppress those feelings forever, and when they do come to the surface, the feeling will cloud all judgement.

Communication anxiety can also oppositely manifest itself without involving any emotion suppression. For instance, let's say your partner unloads only her most powerful feelings and emotions regularly. Some people cannot hold back on certain beliefs, so they lash out, and as a result, both of you end up feeling overwhelmed and confused, leading to another problem. Experiencing these outbursts often enough, you can start feeling that it's your job to find a solution to your partner's issues. It's not enough to notice the anxiety and the strain it's putting on your relationship. You get the feeling you are the sole savior of this partnership. Unfortunately, this usually makes things worse as your partner could start developing resentment towards you for their behavior. We will go into this later on.

Another communication problem is when you consider expressing yourself as a risky affair. Maybe you are wondering what will happen if you reveal what you honestly think. It is enough to trigger your anxiety as you are afraid of the uncertainty of the outcome. Frequently, this symptom stems from not having confidence in yourself and you are worried about an adverse reaction from your partner. In this case, you might be taking a great deal of time to rehearse what you will say and complicate things further by imagining all the possible scenarios.

Also, anxiety can have even worse repercussions if you or your partner will refuse to admit that you are suffering from it. Not acknowledging that there is a problem, especially one as grave as anxiety, will only lead to anger and an irritable behavior that pushes the other person away. Running away from this problem often feels like it's an easier solution, especially by thinking that doing so will shelter the other person. Many people then act based on instinct and don't notice they're avoiding the problem or derailing the discussion by acting irritated. This defensive reaction is almost always caused by anxiety. They don't feel comfortable during the conversation, so they react without even thinking about their behavior, commonly leading to frustration and resentment for both parties.

With that said, now is the time for a little exercise, and you can ask yourself whether you or your partner are exhibiting signs of communication anxiety. The best approach to this little investigation is to take a journal and start making notes of any possible clues. Prepare several lists where you write down what kind of out of place signals you detect in a conversation. Don't just think about your partner, because you might be the problem without even realizing it. Refer to the earlier sections to refresh your memory about the most common symptoms of anxiety and write down any possible sign that comes to mind. You should also take some time to reflect on how you react when you have a conversation with your partner. Think about his or her responses, as well. Finally, you can perform a mental exercise where you think about what you could've done to handle the conversation better. Make a list of the situations where better communication would've prevented any feelings of resentment or anger between the two of you.

Social Situations

Being in certain social situations is difficult for many people who don't even suffer from any form of anxiety. However, those with anxiety will encounter other problems that wouldn't cross other people's minds. It's

26

typical behavior to deny meal invitations from coworkers or friends, ignore unnecessary phone calls, and even avoid small family gatherings. While social situations are more specific and don't occur every day, there are also daily occurrences that can cause extreme amounts of anxiety. For instance, some have issues performing any task or responsibility as long as there's another human being in their presence, looking over their shoulder. In this section, we are going to focus on the broader kind of social situation, referring to any environment in which other people are around.

Isolating yourself from any social situation usually leads to more than just personal social isolation. In some cases, this behavior can turn into a never ending cycle of avoidance. The social aspects of life causing you anxiety, can, in turn, create even more tension in new situations. Avoidance reduces your ability to cope, and you will be dealing with even more fear during the next social gathering. This self-perpetuating cycle often leads to relationship problems, especially breakups, especially if one party is not suffering from any anxiety.

With that in mind, you should take note that a disorder doesn't necessarily cause anxiety in social situations. This problem isn't limited only to those who fit that particular case. Either type of stress can manifest itself in a social setting and determine how you behave when forced to interact with other people, including your partner. For example, your behavior at home may seem normal because you are in a safe space, but in a social event, you may seem unrecognizable to your partner. Your behavior changes as soon as you are around others, especially strangers. Some common signs are stuttering, prolonged silence or pretending you are busy to avoid conversations, talking a lot more than what you may consider "normal", and relying on your partner to carry any conversations. There are also some physical signs that we mentioned earlier when discussing various disorders, such as excessive sweating, nail-biting, playing with an innate object or hair, and avoiding direct eye contact. Some people feel so uncomfortable during social engagements that they leave the conversation suddenly or leave the room altogether.

Once away, the post-anxiety process of overanalyzing everything that happened begins. Most often, the person will obsess over their behavior, if they were likable, talked too much, or if others might have seen them as unintelligent or rude. This kind of behavior can place a great amount of pressure on any relationship as it affects not only your social interaction as a couple but your partner's ability to establish connections and meet new people. In such an example you might even find yourself blaming your partner for your stress and anxiety because he or she placed you in that situation in the first place. This may lead to nothing but resentment and less and less interaction between the two of you.

As mentioned earlier, other disorders can prevent you or your partner from joining any social event. For instance, panic disorder, OCD, and agoraphobia are common afflictions that can prevent anyone's ability to interact with other people without feeling intense anxiety. The reason why social events are so stressful for anyone suffering from anxiety disorder or phobia is too many new elements in which you have no control over. At home, you and your partner have full control over everything that is happening; therefore, there is very little reason to feel anxious. However, at a concert surrounded by thousands of people, you are just one of many and anything can happen, meaning you have nearly no control. As a result, the activities that are comfortable for you to participate in together with your significant other are limited.

How it affects your Relationship

Social interactions are more crucial than ever, and if you (or your partner) are suffering from social anxiety, your career and relationships may suffer as a result. Participating in social gatherings and popular events is essential to developing healthy relationships. Building friendships and expanding your career opportunities can almost exclusively be achieved only in a social setting, whether it's an office Christmas party or someone's birthday.

If you are suffering from anxiety and it makes it impossible for you to socialize with anyone other than your partner, you will unknowingly isolate yourself and feel left out. In addition, your partner will start resenting you for all the pressure you place on him or her whenever you have to avoid a social event. Your partner will always have to come up with an excuse regarding your absence and feel out of place. Keep in mind that after a while some of those people will no longer send invitations to your partner as they can feel that something is wrong, or that they will only receive an excuse instead of attending. In addition, your partner will feel even worse about the entire situation as he or she listens to you blaming yourself and judging yourself over something you have little control. At the same time, if your anxiety does cause a rude overreaction during a social event, your partner will feel torn between siding with her hosts or with you. In either case, unnecessary damage is done to your relationship.

Don't forget that anxiety doesn't always manifest itself in obvious ways. Even if you are the one in the relationship that has it, you might not be aware of how it manipulates some of the decisions you make. For instance, let's say your partner asks you to go to a concert or a party. You don't start talking about your anxiety as you may not even be aware of it at this point. You may refuse the idea because you're just not in the right mood that day, or that you want to spend time at home watching a movie. This scenario will likely repeat itself, slowly increasing the level of frustration building up inside your partner. Why are you acting like this? You may be feeling shameful or guilty because you don't want to disappoint your partner by admitting a problem, so you make up an excuse for not wanting to go out.

In a later chapter we continue this discussion so you learn strategies that will help you "survive" through social events causing anxiety. For now, let's explore an exercise that will help you determine whether your partner is suffering from social anxiety, or whether you are its victim.

Take a piece of paper or in a journal, write down everything you can remember about your behavior in social situations. Do the same thing for your partner. Here are some of the behavioral clues you may notice that are typical for anyone suffering from social anxiety:

1. Avoiding groups of people by sitting alone at the table, standing in a corner or vanishing for certain periods.

2. Making excuses to leave an event as early as possible.

3. Avoiding the conversation by never getting involved even when offered.

4. Suddenly becoming easily irritated and quick to anger.

5. Consuming more alcohol that what is your normal limit under average circumstances. Many people with anxiety feel they need alcohol to survive a social situation or that they even become more likable.

6. Never leaving the side of your more charismatic and talkative partner.

Keep in mind that all of the behaviors above occur only when you or your partner are in a social setting. This is what makes it easy for you to overlook the abnormal behavior. If your partner is the one with the social anxiety, you might accept this behavior because your experience at home is entirely different. However, other noticeable actions can be spotted right before social event or right after it. As mentioned earlier, one of the most common behaviors is to frequently refuse any kind of invitation, especially those that are handed without giving you enough time to prepare psychologically. If you have social anxiety you may also notice that you tend to refuse any offer to go out, even with your partner, by always making up some excuses. Because of the excuses you might not even consider that your choice is made by your anxiety and instead you believe that you simply aren't in the mood for that particular offer.

Consider all of these behaviors and write them down. Writing allows you to process things slower so you can take a deeper look into the various behaviors and reactions. Describe the behavior, feeling, and how you handled the scenario.

Relationship Intimacy Anxiety

Intimacy problems are one of the most common issues relationships encounter. Many couples begin to struggle with sexual activities if they have problems communicating or pre-existing tension that hasn't been worked out and over a prolonged period of stress it can be the reason for a couple to break up. This problem intensifies if anxiety is present.

Let's analyze this situation by starting from the most basic level. The purpose of sex is to produce children that perpetuate the species. Naturally, for the first years, many couples aren't focused on this; however, this doesn't stop human nature. In any case, your body responds to sexual signals and behaviors when you are in a safe place. If you're suffering from constant anxiety, you will need to prepare your mind in such a way that your body relaxes and enough to be ready for a pleasurable intimate experience. You might have to start with various relaxation techniques to place your mind into a safe environment and eliminate all of your thoughts of anxiety.

A variety of reasons cause sexual anxiety, and they are all specific. If you or your partner feel anxious when it comes to sex, it might be due to the following:

1. A past childhood trauma.

2. Lack of confidence and feeling physically unattractive.

3. Past religious beliefs are affecting the way you look at sexual intimacy.

4. Fear regarding your bedroom performance.

31

There are plenty of other reasons, however experiencing just one of these is more than enough to put a strain on any relationship. Luckily most of these problems can be controlled or even resolved with therapy. With the root causes of sexual anxiety in mind, let's take a look at some behaviors that may be too subtle for you to notice. Keep in mind that you might not realize that your actions are getting in the way of a healthy relationship. The brain is tricky sometimes.

Certain behaviors can indicate either you or your partner are suffering from sexual intimacy anxiety and that is why the bedroom department is suffering. For instance, a common indicator is when one of you makes an excuse to go to bed earlier than usual. Of course, refusing sex or saying that you are too tired for it doesn't always mean that it is caused by deeper issues. But if you find yourself often making excuses to avoid physical intimacy with your partner, then you are probably having some sexual anxiety problems.

Sexual anxiety has different effects on men and women. For instance, most men with this problem will have an issue maintaining an erection during intercourse, fail to have an orgasm or experience premature ejaculation. Women, on the other hand, can suffer from physical pain during sex and they usually fail to climax. In both cases these issues lead to more anxiety and frustration within the relationship.

Keep in mind that a great deal of people go through some feelings of anxiety when it comes to sex, however they all do around the same age. It's a part of biology, as discussed earlier, and a small amount of anxiety can be beneficial. However, there are people suffering from real intimacy anxiety, and just the thought of being close to someone is enough to cause so much stress they never try. Here are some examples of what people stress about if they are afflicted with this kind of anxiety:

1. Worrying about being seen naked is a common issue. A lot of people think they are too fat, ugly or in some way physically unattractive. This self-doubt and lack of confidence lead to a bad

experience that, in turn, causes more anxiety directly affecting intimacy.

2. A person mistreated in their childhood or experiencing sexually abuse can leave lasting scars. The scars of this trauma can survive for a long time, and these people often consider themselves "damaged" and nobody will ever want to be intimate with them.

3. The inability to sexually pleasure a partner by bringing her to climax is a concern that mostly afflicts men. A great deal of men are brought up to think that if they fail to pleasure a woman then they are not "real men." Therefore they see themselves as failures and become too afraid to engage in future sexual activities due to this fear of failing.

4. The fear of abandonment can also lead to intimacy anxiety, especially when it comes to women. The thought of refusing intercourse produces an overwhelming fear that their partner will leave and find someone else. This leads to intimacy that isn't pleasurable for the woman, and in the end, results in relationship problems as the anxiety only gets worse.

There is no denying that sex is vital to a relationship, no matter how young or old the couple is. Having such thoughts and behaviors regarding intimacy as described above, can cause damage to a relationship. In a later chapter, we will discuss various techniques that will help bring you or your partner relief from sexual anxiety.

How it affects your Relationship

Let's say your partner suffered some kind of sexual trauma in his or her past. This means that being intimate with something is challenging at best, if not impossible. Even well-established relationships that have developed over several years can suffer from the anxiety that this trauma causes. It's good to keep in mind that it's not your fault and you can't put the blame on your partner either. Someone who suffered from a sexual trauma usually requires time, safety and the guidance of a professional therapist in order to navigate these troubled waters. However, undergoing therapy won't solve the problem overnight. On the contrary, if your partner seeks help to explore past issues there may be an even more significant drop in sexual activity during that time. You should still be careful because if the libido doesn't waiver eventually, it can create a separate issue that affects you both. If you find yourself in this situation, you should sit down with your partner and have an honest discussion about what is happening, or try couple's therapy.

Those affected by OCD can encounter extreme issues with being intimate. They are often afraid of sex, can't feel any pleasure from it, or they are disgusted even at the mere thought of it. If you or your partner are in this situation, therapy is an invaluable resource and there is medication available.

Medications for anxiety sometimes have the unpleasant side effects of lowering libido or ultimately killing the urge to have sex. So your partner may be able to get aroused, but an orgasm doesn't happen. Some people even lose all of their desire of being intimate. If you do notice a significant drop in your partner's libido, you should keep the discussion open, as it may be a side effect. Keep in mind that while many of these prescribed medications are necessary to treat various disorders, doctors don't always mention a possible change in sexual performance. Therefore you should pay attention to any significant change in yourself or your partner, because a great deal of people suffering from anxiety are too afraid to mention this personal problem to a doctor. For instance, imagine someone with extreme social anxiety going to the doctor's office to admit bedroom issues. This is why an additional push from your partner is required. If your partner feels this way, you should provide words of encouragement to help him or her speak up because doctors hear about these issues all the time, and they are trained to handle them professionally. This is especially important because in most cases an adjustment to the dosage is all that is needed.

Now that you know more about this type of anxiety, it's time to work on a sexual anxiety exercise

Start by simply thinking about your relationship. By using a scale from one to ten you should consider how good your sex life is. One means that there is no intimacy present anymore, and ten means that you are perfectly happy with the way things are. Assign a grade to your level of satisfaction. Next, grab a piece of paper and create two lists which will contain the positive parts of your sex life, as well as the negative. In the first list, write down things like "sex is enjoyable," while in the second list, you write something like "my partner always has an excuse not to make love." Once both lists are complete, you can determine how much your relationship is affected by this key issue. If you are the one not satisfying your partner, you should examine your behavior and decide how often you turn him or her down. You may also want to give this list to your partner to fill out in order to see a different point of view and then have a healthy discussion about it.

Emotion Control

Remember the last time somebody asked you how you're feeling? You probably answered with "I'm good" or something along those lines, even though you were probably worrying about something or you were angry. We restrain ourselves from being truthful about our feelings because it's the norm. Society doesn't expect us to behave in any other way than what is deemed acceptable. For instance, when you were younger, you probably received a pair of socks or a sweater from someone for your birthday. That probably didn't make you happy or grateful, especially as a kid wanting toys and things to play with. However, you pretended to like it no matter your true feelings because that's how you were supposed to.

The problem develops when we get older. Most of these social rules and behaviors are still valid, but now they have become a real source of anxiety for many people. Why? Simply because we become more self-aware once we mature and we start worrying about others not accepting our thoughts, ideas, or feelings. If you find yourself in this situation, you might be fueling a vicious cycle without even knowing. For example, you might stress about your partner, finding out how you truly feel about something abnormal. As a result, you start suppressing that feeling as much as you can, and it keeps growing more and more, forcing you to adapt your suppression techniques. You end up wasting a great deal of energy on maintaining this cycle.

More common examples of feelings most people find socially unacceptable to display out in the open are fear, anger, and sadness. As you probably already know, if you are suffering from anxiety, your emotions have a far stronger impact on your wellbeing. In other words, what makes someone only slightly angry can provoke even rage and violent behavior in those suffering from various anxiety disorders. The other problem is the fact that most people with anxiety aren't fully aware of their feelings, and they lack an understanding of them. Having acceptance issues towards your emotions can lead to a severe lack of control. Therefore, if your partner is angry about something, they might not fully comprehend the feeling and as a result, won't know how to act. This lack of understanding can result in a severe reaction, or overreaction, making everything worse and damaging the relationship.

People that are more sensitive to emotions tend to react to their environment as if it isn't safe for them. The same thing happens to those who are always anxious and worried because their mental focus is on potential danger. Not all of those who are emotional experience a great deal of anxiety; however, fear is commonly linked to emotional sensitivity. The main factors that influence this relationship are the environment in which you were brought up and your genes. Certain people are born to react with far more emotion to circumstances that won't even influence others. Even if they learn how to control or manipulate their thoughts and reactions, they will never be able to ignore their sensitivity.

The environment has the most influence on someone when growing up. At this point, a person is still developing and highly susceptible to negative experiences and traumas. Let's say your partner learned from their parents how to look at emotions from a calm and rational point of view and knows that hunger or fatigue causes irritability. On the other hand, if you are repeatedly told by those raising you that what you feel is wrong, or in your head, you are very likely to develop a form of anxiety. If this behavior isn't corrected, you could grow up with mixed and confusing feelings. Your understanding of emotions and dealing with them appropriately will continue to be stunted throughout your adult life.

With all the above in mind, let's discuss how difficulties with emotion control and regulation can damage your relationship.

How it affects your Relationship

Communication in a relationship can be quite challenging and stressful at times if you or your partner are suppressing your feelings and don't display your genuine\ emotions. The most basic example of this is when you ask your partner what he's angry or upset, and he replies with the classic "I'm fine." Obviously, in this case, it's rather difficult to improve or fix the situation when you can't even get through to your partner. At the same time, however, your partner may also be the type who changes his mood often. Going from one state of mind to another multiple times a week or even a day makes communication even more difficult. Keep in mind a lot of these cases imply the existence of another disorder on top of the anxiety. Also, your partner may occasionally have emotional outbursts or unnecessarily overreact to a situation. In any of these scenarios, communication becomes close to impossible and you might make things worse in the relationship.

Another result of not being able to regulate your emotions has to deal with jealousy and insecurity. For example, if your partner gets suspicious easily and is uncertain about himself. In the case of jealousy, you would have to spend your energy to comforting him and proving nothing is going on, and he shouldn't feel this way. In the case of insecurity, it can be even more exhausting as he will always seek your reassurance on anything, which will test your patience. A sign that both of these issues have in common is clinginess. Whether jealous or insecure, your partner is likely to become clingy and never giving you enough time for yourself. These actions lead to feeling suffocated, a sense of lost identity, and annoyance because you're never alone since you always have to deal with their faults. If you are with someone who can't control his or her emotions, it's easy to feel helpless, and nothing you do is right. Your partner's affliction can easily make you spiral into your very own cycle of anxiety or even depression.

If you are having trouble determining the subtle signs of emotional instability, whether in your partner or yourself, you can work on this exercise to find out. All you need to do is visualize the time when you or your partner felt anxious but without expressing it directly. Write down on a piece of paper the dialogue of that specific situation and the actions taken as a response. That should be a clear sign. You can spend some time thinking of any other cases where anxiety is involved.

Anxiety at Work

It's common for people suffering from anxiety to need to take time off from work because of it. Especially those with general anxiety disorder, however, most of them never list this as their reason for requiring the break. In most cases, these people are afraid of the repercussions if their boss finds out about their anxiety problems because work performance is often affected by them.

As you can see, what we have so far is a perfect example of a vicious cycle that stems from anxiety. People stress about how their job performance is influenced by fear, which leads to even more anxiety and as a result, may impact their productivity.

Keep in mind that general anxiety disorder isn't the only culprit when it comes to work-related anxiety issues. Imagine someone with panic disorder going to work daily with the fear of suffering a panic attack in front of his colleagues or boss looming over his shoulders. This type of person limits his or her career path because they would choose a position that doesn't require working with others.

At the same time, people with OCD would encounter difficulties in finishing various tasks simply because they never feel that what they're doing is good enough. Their work is never perfect, so they try to tweak every possible detail. As a result, they miss important deadlines, and suffer extreme anxiety when work undergoes evaluation.

People with various phobias would have to give up a variety of career opportunities because of fear. Imagine someone with an extreme fear of heights working in an office on the 15th floor of a building. Or someone with anxiety of bridges finding their dream job is on the other side of a vast river. With the phobia controlling you, you would have to pass up the opportunity as the anxiety of crossing that bridge every day would be too much.

These situations pose a challenge for those who suffer with anxiety as they are unable to fulfill their dreams or reach their full potential. If your partner is in any of these situations, he or she might experience some relief from having a routine, predictable job, however, over time this can change into a feeling of worthlessness as others are progressing in their fields. There is always another side of this coin, as some people with anxiety turn into workaholics. Who either work too much or invest too much time in achieving up to their own standards, which can be impossibly high. Plenty of people on this end of the spectrum feel that they can't rely on anyone else other than themselves, they are extremely worried about evaluation periods, and they can't keep up with deadlines. Causing them to spend extra hours at the office to compensate for missed assignments. If you find yourself in this situation, your quality of life is without a doubt affected, and your relationship may suffer because of the excessive amount of work you are doing.

How it affects your Relationship

Work is a necessity for most; therefore, it's an obligation that is unavoidable like other situations causing anxiety. If you are experiencing stress at work, you will most likely bring it with home and into your relationship. Separating work from home life can be difficult for even those who are unafflicted. You may also have trouble finding the motivation to go back to work the next day because you know that by doing so, you will suffer from even more anxiety. These issues are another example of the self-perpetuating cycle of anxiety. Every worry that you have due to your work life will start affecting the quality of your sleep, eating habits, and the relationship with your partner. Performance anxiety is a prevalent issue, and it can have a severe impact on work-life balance. As you invest more effort in attempting to stay afloat or get ahead of colleagues, the result is less time spent with your partner. It quickly leads to feelings of neglect and a build-up of frustration as distance forms between you and your mate.

In extreme cases, some people suffer from so much anxiety that they cannot seek employment. For instance, any of the various disorders we discussed earlier can prevent you from participating in a job interview because the interaction with a potential employer can be too stressful. You may worry about your interview performance, your physical appearance, your ability to answer the questions appropriately, and so on. Even if you push yourself to go to the interview, you may not get the position. Displaying apparent anxiety or a lack of self-confidence right off the bat can seem issues to an employer. This issue would lead to a financially troubled relationship as having only one income will affect your life as a couple. Even if that income is enough to live comfortably, most people start developing some resentment when they are the only ones supporting the house economically.

The situation can continue to decline if your anxiety prevents you from performing other tasks that aren't work-related. Let's say you, as a couple, have made peace with the fact that you cannot work. You may not have the ability to perform other kinds of tasks either, and therefore, your partner would have to take on even more responsibilities. Eventually the relationship would become unsustainable as other issues would emerge over time, and your partner would slowly start feeling resentful, frustrated, and angry.

Let's take a look at an exercise you can do to determine whether you or your partner, are affected by work-related anxiety. Start by taking into consideration whether one of you is experiencing anything we discussed earlier, and then write down any work-related behaviors, worries, and so on. Here are some of the questions you can ask yourself:

1. Are you currently employed, or do you consider yourself to be occupying a position that is beneath your education, skill, and experience? As mentioned earlier, anxiety can easily make you satisfied with any steady, routine-filled job you became accustomed to overtime, so give this some thought.

2. Does your anxiety force you to skip a few work days due to the symptoms you experience? Being anxious and worried all the time can be extremely tiresome.

3. Are you considering quitting your current job, or quitting work in general due to all the problems it causes? It's normal for people to want to change a position they aren't satisfied with. However, those with anxiety can randomly quit because they are overwhelmed by their symptoms. If you can answer this question with a solid yes, what is the exact reason for doing so? You need to determine what holds you back, what keeps you from

41

succeeding. You need to ask yourself whether it's because of financial reasons, the anxiety of changing jobs, not having enough growth opportunities, etc.

Take the time to write everything down as seeing your thoughts in writing gives you a different perspective and allows you to process your emotions more objectively. Write all of the situations you can think of, what you felt at the time and your whole reasoning process that has led to your final decision.

Parenting with Anxiety

Being in a relationship while affected by anxiety is difficult but having children under the same circumstances can be genuinely challenging. Keep in mind that children can make parents however, those who are naturally anxious or suffer from a disorder will obsess over the safety of the child before it is even born. It is normal to feel a certain amount of concern for your children, whether it's for their health or security reasons. Many parents continue worrying about their kids even when they are fully matured and starting families of their own. Relationships change when children enter the picture. Various relationship anxieties may start developing, even ones that were never there before.

The term "helicopter parent," refers to parents always worried about their children and come to their aid at the first sign of distress. These parents usually experience intense anxiety because of all the fears that manifest when children are around. These parents obsess over their kids' safety and will aggressively seek to control every aspect of their lives to keep them safe and feel nurtured. However, there are other parenting-related anxiety symptoms out there, such as:

1. Criticizing your children no matter how well they do. This issue

can even continue into the child's adult life, as the parents will continue criticizing his decisions and lifestyle. Keep in mind that "normal" parents will be critical regarding their children as well, but not on the same level as those who suffer from an anxiety disorder.

2. Some parents fail to display enough affection due to their anxiety. They don't smile as often as they should, and they always expect something to go wrong, which leads to even more worries and more stress.

3. Being inclined to ignore a child's opinion or completely disrespect and even mock his or her point of view. These parents sometimes fail to encourage independent critical thinking.

As previously mentioned, none of this means that only parents suffering from various anxiety disorders are anxious when it comes to their children. There are many reasons to be worried, and most of them are due to the lack of control parents feel. If you find yourself worrying about your children all the time or stress over future children, you could limit the kind of activities your family participates. Many such parents think that they protect their children by excluding them from potentially dangerous situations when they are average, safe social settings. Behavior like this can be caused by anxiety, in some cases, and it is incredibly damaging for the parents and child. Now let's take a look at how parenting anxiety can even affect your romantic relationship.

How it affects your Relationship

As already mentioned, anxiety can severely impact your approach to parenting and the development of your children. However, your partner may also be affected if you are displaying an overprotective behavior. Preventing your children from participating in social events with other children, allowing them to explore their surroundings and interests only inhibits their growth and ability to learn. Your partner may have a different view on child upbringing or education and disagree with what you find acceptable. This conflict in your relationship can ultimately affect your parenting and the child's development.

If your anxiety is causing so much friction between members of the family, think of the age-old words of letting kids be kids. Don't forget that anxiety is all about dangers you perceive and imagine, and this doesn't automatically turn them into reality. The threat of your child getting hurt may seem real, and you may think you couldn't handle your emotions if something happened to them. It's fairly common for parents to overreact after a child gets hurt during an activity. Imagine your kid is playing soccer with his friends and he breaks his leg in the process. After such a high energy event, you will be tempted never to let him play soccer with his friends again because it's too dangerous.

Now let's discuss more the conflict between you and your partner when one of you has a different opinion on parenting due to anxiety. Imagine the following scenario: your child wants to take his bike and go to his best friend's house, which is around half an hour away. He wants to go alone, of course, without a parent escorting him. Your partner knows where the friend lives and the route is perfectly safe, so he says yes and lets the kid go on his own. However, your answer to his wish is a resounding "no." He then goes to the seemingly more "reasonable" parent to get another confirmation and leaves. At this point, the child has established that one parent is much easier to convince and is more accepting of his plans, opinions, and wishes. The problem however, is that you are now probably feeling anger or resentment towards your partner for not agreeing with you and going against your decision. In addition, you may also be experiencing even more anxiety because the thought of your child leaving on his own is frightening.

While always being on the same page with your partner is hard, they should be aware and understand your anxiety can impact decision making, especially when it comes to parenting. Both of you need to invest additional time in communicating with each other and learning how to compromise in various situations. You need to work together despite your anxiety because you're on the same team no matter what. If the two of you already are parents, you should take a step back and figure out all the differences and similarities you find regarding your parenting methods.

As an exercise, you should think about the upbringing of your children and the way you are going to raise them. You need to decide how willing the two of you are to allow your children to explore new things and how much freedom you offer them to be independent. Both of you should write down a list of all the situations you can think about and then write down how you would handle them. Once you have the answers, you can compare them to see the differences between your partner's parenting style and yours as well. You should pay attention to which parent the child seeks permission from when it comes to risky activities. For instance, if you are very anxious and protective of the child, he may seek your partner's approval when it comes to sports or going camping. Think of any such examples and write them down to discuss things with your partner.

Lastly, you should think about the way you react to any situation that involves your child and write down your behavior. You should then compare your actions to those of your partner's. Pay special attention to the circumstances that led to your child being hurt. Whether it's physical while playing a sport, or emotionally by being embarrassed or bullied at school. Write down everything you can think of, and discuss it with your partner. Communication is key.

Chapter 3: Negative Core Beliefs

Core beliefs are the beliefs we have about ourselves, about others and the world around us; they have been in place since childhood, evolving from past experiences. They stick with people their entire lives, as a mechanism that helps them predict new situations. Due to these beliefs we know how to behave and respond in various scenarios.

These beliefs can be positive and negative. In other words, if you had positive experiences in the past, your views will also be positive. For example, if you grew up with parents who loved each other and did not hide it, you will have a positive view on love. You will seek out a partner who fits into the picture of a perfect relationship, based on what your parents imprinted on you.

However, if you grew up with negative experiences like one of your parents abandoning your family, chances are you will grow up with a negative belief in all relationships. You may have a core belief in abandonment, which makes you afraid of your partner leaving you, and your behavior reflects the fear in negative ways. This behavior, in turn, will continue to hurt your relationship. The beliefs you have determine how you see yourself. To what extent do you believe yourself to be worthy, competent, powerful, safe and loved. The negative thoughts you have about yourself, others, and the world are damaging to relationships and should be dealt with accordingly.

Since core beliefs have their roots in the early stages of human development, they are very challenging to overcome, but not impossible. They are seen as absolute truths about oneself, others, and the world. When triggered, negative beliefs can cause strong emotions that make you feel shame, depression, loss, anger, and more. There are two ways of overcoming these beliefs. One is better management of the situations that trigger them, and the other is to manage behavioral reactions that follow.

As mentioned, our beliefs come from our childhood, which often means we continue to thin like a child even in adulthood. Ignoring consequences, we favor instant gratification instead of looking at the long term outcome. We also rely on stereotypes and prejudices developed during childhood. We often react based on our emotions, and we do not use objectivism and logic to observe our situation. We are aggressive, vengeful, and we don't listen to others. To learn how to behave and not trigger these negative beliefs, we have to understand them by thoroughly understanding the positive and negative that apply to us.

Identifying your Beliefs

Core beliefs work on an unconscious level, and this makes them hard to identify. People are often not aware of them, as they hide deep in the subconscious mind, and they are believed to be part of the basic survival instinct and defense mechanisms. However, if you don't make the effort to become aware of these beliefs and accept them, you will never be able to change your behavior, thus your relationships will continue to be influenced, or even ruined by them.

There are many ways to identify which beliefs you possess. Cognitive-behavioral therapy can test your views, or you can explore them by following the *downward arrow technique*. This means that when a thought pops into your head, you will have to examine it and follow it backwards all the way to the point where it originated. Here is an example:

Let's say you think you are lazy. Ask yourself what does that mean and what does it tell you. You will come to discover that you procrastinate too much, and it is because you think you will fail anyway, so why even bother. Ask yourself again. What does this mean about you? You could come up with an answer such as "I am weak" or "I am not competent enough." Continue asking yourself "what does this mean about me" until you have no more answers. The last one you came up with is your core belief. In this case, it might be that you do not think you are good enough.

There are many negative core beliefs, but let's label the most common ones. They often come in the form of a thought that sounds similar to the following:

1. I am not good enough.

2. I am unlovable.

3. I am incompetent.

4. I am unsure.

5. I am always wrong.

6. I am defective.

7. I am powerless.

8. I have no value.

You may notice that all of these phrases start with "I am." They are negative core beliefs that you have about yourself. When you try to predict how others feel about you, or what they think about you, it is called having a supportive belief. For example:

1. Nobody loves me.

2. Nobody supports me.

3. Nobody thinks I can do it.

4. Everyone thinks I'm stupid.

5. Everyone believes I'm incompetent.

Supportive beliefs are not real core beliefs. They are there to reinforce them instead. In other words, when your core beliefs tell you "I am unlovable" thoughts such as "nobody loves me" are there to support it.

Once you have identified your negative core beliefs, you can start working on overcoming them.

How Negative Beliefs Affect your Relationships

Negative beliefs influence the way we start a new relationship, but they also change the way we maintain the existing ones.

The most common beliefs that influence romantic relationships are the belief of abandonment, emotional deprivation, insecurity, and failure. We often see them as follows:

1. My loved one will abandon me.

2. My loved one will hurt me.

3. My loved one doesn't love me back.

4. My loved one will not protect me.

5. My loved one will see how unlovable I am.

Core beliefs are triggered because you find yourself in situations that unconsciously remind you of past experiences. Negative core beliefs are easy to trigger because they are based on fear. The behavior that follows them is the one that will determine how your relationship will be affected. Such beliefs can make you irrational, dependent, clingy, and make you lash out in anger. All these behaviors may influence a relationship in a negative way, and they must be changed. Don't expect your partner to be responsible for the way you react in certain situations; it is your duty to work on happiness. You can't rely on your partner to repair the situation, to mind your feelings, and be cautious not to trigger your unfavorable ideas. Your partner is human too, and he is dealing with his own set of negative thoughts, emotions, and beliefs.

Overcoming Negative Beliefs

We already mentioned that there are two ways of overcoming core beliefs, and in this section, we will discuss how to do it and what results we should expect.

Managing your Situation

Negative beliefs are triggered by specific situations, conversations, as well as people, and the point is to keep them from influencing the choices you make in your relationship. They will be the determining factor of what type of personality one might possess that you find attractive. Based on your past experiences, you might find it easy to attach yourself to individual personalities that often trigger core beliefs. This is how your mind distorts reality and makes wrong attachment figures attractive. A person with abandonment beliefs was attached during childhood to a figure who abandoned him. This person will find people who have a predisposition to leave him to be the most attractive ones and will seek them as partners. It is essential to make a conscious decision not to attach yourself to people who trigger your beliefs often. Here is a list of possible personalities that will trigger your own core beliefs:

1. Abandoner: This person is most likely already involved in a relationship with someone else. He or she is also unpredictable, unable to commit, and doesn't have a set plan for the future. They are not very supportive, and they are often unavailable exactly when you need them.

2. Abuser: They will lie, manipulate, and cheat. They are untrustworthy and unsafe. They will abuse you emotionally or physically. They will harm you and make you feel like you deserve it as if you are the one to blame for everything.

3. Depriver: They will avoid forming an attachment to you. They will close themselves off emotionally and have little value for your life together. They will often be unable to give you the relationship you are longing for.

4. Judge: This is the type of personality that will always judge your achievements, thoughts, and emotions. He will find flaws in you and will expose them to others. He will disrespect you and think you are not good enough for him.

5. Critic: They will compare you to themselves and to others, they will criticize your every move and they will make you feel incompetent.

Avoid these types of personalities, and you will successfully avoid the negative situations they will put you in. It makes a difference if someone is triggering your core beliefs more frequently or once in a while. We all have various beliefs and they will eventually be triggered unintentionally by others, but if it happens rarely, or on occasion, this person might still be worth your attention, and with work, both of you can find happiness in a fruitful relationship.

Managing your Behavior

It is vital that you are perfectly aware of what negative core beliefs you possess so you will recognize them when they are triggered. Once it is triggered, there is no more time to avoid the situation. The only thing you can do is try to properly manage your reactions and behaviors. Try writing down what you were doing when your ideals were triggered, how did you behave, and what actions did you take. For example, let's say you have a failure belief, meaning you are always afraid of not being good enough. You find yourself in a situation where your partner is giving you constructive criticism. It can be something as simple as proposing how to improve your recipe for a special dessert. Your belief is triggered, and you

51

start comparing yourself to others, maybe to his mother's cooking abilities. You might react by avoiding the discussion, or you might begin criticizing your partner in return. To change your behavior and outbursts, you must recognize your positive core values, and try your best to focus on them.

Core values are principals we hold in high regard, and we do our best to live by them. They can be honesty, faith, commitment, loyalty, optimism, courage, and so on. Ask yourself what are yours and write them down. You need to practice your core values as often as possible. Next time your negative beliefs are triggered, try to react with your values in mind. Instead of avoiding the discussion, be courageous, and confront it. Instead of criticizing others when you feel angry, remind yourself how highly you value peace and respond calmly and logically.

Practice this behavior every day. Put yourself in situations where your values can come to light. Volunteer, help others, and offer support. The more practice you have when your core beliefs are stable, the better you will respond once they are not.

Chapter 4: Toxic Relationships

Anxiety isn't always the element which affects a relationship. Sometimes it's the other way around, and the reason you have anxiety is because of a toxic relationship. But what exactly does toxic mean? We refer to a relationship as toxic when it isn't beneficial to you and it's harmful in some way. The building blocks for a healthy relationship are made from mutual respect and admiration, but sometimes it just isn't enough.

However, there is a difference between a problematic relationship and a toxic one, and that is mainly the noxious atmosphere that surrounds you. This kind of relationship can suffocate you with time and prevent you from living a happy, productive life. Many factors lead to toxicity. It is most often caused by friction that can occur between two people that are opposites of each other. In others, nothing specific is to blame, and the toxic relationship grows from the lack of communication, the establishment of boundaries and the ability to agree on something, or at the very least compromise.

Take not that not all toxic relationships develop because of the couple. Sometimes there is an outlier seeking to influence conflict because they will benefit from it in some way. This type of individual preys on other people's insecurities, weaknesses, or manipulates his way inside a relationship from which he has something to gain. In some cases, a toxic person seeks to destroy a relationship in order to get closer to one of them. He or she may not even be aware of their damaging behavior because of a self-obsessed focus that does not extend to anyone else. Personal needs, emotions, and goals take priority over anyone else's wellbeing.

With that in mind, let's briefly explore the characteristics of a toxic relationship:

1. Poisonous: A relationship that is extremely unpleasant to be around as it poisons the atmosphere around it. It makes anyone around the couple anxious, and it can even lead to psychological

and emotional problems such as anxiety and depression.

2. Deadly: Toxic relationships are bad for your health. In many cases, it involved risky, destructive, and abusive behaviors. Some people end up harming themselves with alcohol, drugs, or worse. Injuries and even death can become the final result.

3. Negative: In this kind of relationship, negativity is the norm. There is no positive reinforcement, even when children are involved. The overwhelming lack of approval and emotional support is standard.

4. Harmful: Toxic relationships lack balance and awareness. Those involved are never truly aware of each other and lack the most positive principles that a healthy relationship needs. Toxicity also promotes immoral and malicious acts that harm a romantic relationship.

What we have discussed so far may lead you to think that toxic people are psychopaths and nothing more. While it is true that some of them are, that's not always the case. However, psychopaths are expert manipulators due to their ability to mask their true feelings and intentions. These people have a psychological disorder that makes their personality imposing, pretentious, and even impulsive. Many aren't aware of their behavior and the effects it has on others. They tend to be self-absorbed and expect a great deal from others while being narcissistic and deceitful. In other words, they lack insight as well as empathy. Psychopaths are people who seek attention, admiration, and acceptance, but they will need to accept their responsibilities and the needs of others.

Why and how would anyone end up in a relationship with someone who displays psychopathic traits? The answer lies in their ability to maintain appearances and manipulate others. If they realize you see through their charade, they will do anything to convince you that they are a good person. They may start doing good deeds, not out of empathy and love, but out of the need to redeem themselves. In many cases, these people can recover if their psychopathic disorder isn't too severe. With help, they can gain control over themselves and their toxic behavior, so they can live a productive life without hurting others in the process.

As mentioned earlier, toxic relationships don't always involve psychopaths or those who display similar traits. In many situations, these relationships are the way they are due to decent people that are terrible decision-makers, or that lack social skills. Taking a wrong turn in life happens to everyone, and many people change but not always for the better.

Warning Signs

Now that you can better identify toxic relationships and the kind of people that are involved let's see if you're in one or not. Humans are complex creatures, and the traits we discussed don't necessarily make someone toxic. Some underlying issues and disorders can make people behave negatively. However, they can still be excellent partners. With that said, here's a list of questions you can ask yourself to learn more about your relationship:

1. How do you feel in the company of your partner?

2. Do you feel happy, safe, and nurtured in the presence of your significant other?

3. Are all the other people involved in your relationship safe and happy? For instance your children (if you have any), parents, friends and so on. As mentioned earlier, people tend to avoid toxic relationships instead of being in contact with them.

4. Do you experience anxiety or panic attacks when you are about to discuss something with your partner?

5. Can you think of any scenarios in which you were manipulated to

do something that wasn't for your best interest?

6. Is your partner pushing the limits of what you would consider ethical? Is he or she even crossing the line of what is legal?

7. Does your partner to push you to perform challenging tasks that you consider entirely unnecessary? These challenges may seem pointless, and that you need to resolve just because it's what your partner wants.

8. Do you feel emotionally strained and exhausted after interacting with your partner?

If you can answer a few of these questions, you are likely in a toxic relationship that may be making you anxious and damaging your health. You then need to decide for yourself whether you wish to stay in this kind of relationship to repair it or leave. If you do decide to stay, there's a series of decisions you need to make. For instance, you need to feel in control with the idea of resisting all the negativity that comes with a toxic partner, because you will need to endure feelings of anxiety and stress. You need to ask yourself whether you are gaining enough from that relationship and whether it's worth sacrificing yourself for it.

Handling a Toxic Relationship

As mentioned, a toxic relationship can be a powerful source of anxiety. It doesn't have to be a romantic relationship either. Some of them you can avoid by cutting contact with some people to feel relief. However, there are certain people you simply cannot break away from, whether they are romantic partners or your mother in law. This is why in this section we are going to discuss how to deal with such a relationship.

The first step is to accept the inescapable situation. When your options

56

are limited, you cannot achieve relief by avoidance, and acceptance leads to a decrease in anxiety. You may be tempted to be hostile towards that person, but it won't help. Instead, it will just add to your worries and stress. At this point, your only alternative is managing your anxiety by admitting to yourself that you may never be able to get along with that person. In addition, you can attempt to ignore him or her completely by never going spending time together and ignoring any contact. However, none of these tactics usually work.

Resistance can help short-term, but it will continue generating anxiety and stress because the toxic person knows how to get under your skin and take advantage of you. Accept that this relationship is difficult and challenges you but you are doing your best to make it better. That doesn't mean you should completely surrender. By accepting your situation, you will allow yourself new possibilities and new options instead of repeatedly punishing yourself.

Take note that for the process of acceptance to take hold, you need to be consciously aware that you are not responsible for anyone else's emotions and reactions. Toxic behavior often makes people blame you for their situation and feelings. Do not accept any of that, as you are not the reason for their suffering. They need to take responsibility for their thoughts and actions instead of blaming others.

The second step is telling the truth. If a toxic relationship is creating stress, likely, you often lie to avoid conflict, which causes even more anxiety. The problem is that when you lie to such a person, you enable them and become partially responsible for the reality they create — leading to the toxic environment surrounding them.

For instance, let's say you intentionally didn't invite the problematic person to your birthday. When confronted about it, you may be tempted to say that you sent an invitation but used the wrong address, or it went into the spam folder. Lying isn't easy, especially if you are an anxious person. People can tell, especially if you tend to make excuses for yourself often enough. Instead of lying you should tell the truth, and the real truth. This means that you shouldn't use an excuse. just say they make you uncomfortable and extremely anxious, that is why you didn't invite them. Telling the truth can be difficult and even painful because it affects others. It takes a great deal of courage and once you get through the experience, you will feel a powerful sense of relief. In the end, it's better to get something off your chest instead of carrying it.

Chapter 5: Relationship Obsessive-Compulsive Disorder

Relationship obsessive-compulsive disorder (ROCD) is also known as Relationship Substantiation, a subcategory of OCD. It manifests when a person is consumed by doubts about a relationship. Most people recognize it during big relationship milestones such as moving in together or when they are about to get married. And if there is even a little doubt whether their partner is the right one or whether their marriage will last, it can cause the person to spiral.

OCD is known for having its ups and downs, and you might not even be aware about it as people are often quick to disregard what troubles them. Usually, OCD is triggered when a big change happens or is about to happen. Marriage is one of these huge changes and that is why ROCD might come to life at that moment.

A person who suffers from ROCD often question his partner's motivation as well as his own. He must be sure that they are perfect for each other and he will obsess about it. He often thinks "Who will guarantee to me that he/she is the one" and he will constantly search for evidence to support the claim that his partner is the right choice. Such a person will continuously ask his family and friends if they like his or her partner, and he will exhaust himself by reading articles about the perfect relationship, just to acknowledge that his is fitting the picture.

Most people eagerly talk about a marriage planned for the future, but as the date nears, they can start questioning the relationship. Coming up with reasons why they aren't a good match, delaying the marriage to be able to find more proof that the choice is right. By no means does this mean that he or she doesn't love you anymore. ROCD happens for various reasons, and it's not always due to a lack of love.

Relationship OCD is no different from any other subcategory of OCD. They are all the product of intrusive thoughts that demand clarification, order, and confirmation. Most of the couples have similar thoughts and it is normal to question your relationship from time to time. It is completely normal to feel different levels of attraction towards your partner during your relationship. ROCD is diagnosed in people whose anxiousness is triggered by such thoughts and whose connection is literally hijacked by and no longer functioning correctly.

There are two types of ROCD that we can distinguish. One concentrates on the relationship, and the other is on your partner. Keep in mind that both types can occur at the same time. No matter which one you have, your ordinary life can be interrupted with the same intensity. When focused on the relationship R-OCD can make you question whether your partner is the right one, or if the relationship will last, and if it will be happy and healthy. However, if it is focused on your partner, you might question his or her abilities and personality. You might wonder whether your partner is intelligent, attractive, or capable enough for your standards.

Symptoms

The difference between occasional and chronic doubt in a relationship is that everyone experiences it, it's just if ROCD is manifesting itself as a response to intrusive thoughts. A person suffering from this affliction will perform repetitive, ritualistic actions that are considered compulsive to relieve anxiety.

These are the most common symptoms of ROCD:

1. Seeking constant reassurance about your relationship or partner: compulsively asking others their opinion and views on your relationship. You may even want to ask your partner what they think about the relationship and love.

2. Seeking evidence: An OCD person often needs evidence confirming that this is the right one. In other words, he needs

proof that love is real. He will compulsively question himself whether he is attracted to his partner enough, to validate the relationship.

3. Extreme comparison: Compulsively comparing your partner to your ex or someone else in general. Some people can even go so far as comparing the relationship to a fictional one from a movie, or book.

4. Another symptom of ROCD is the constant probing of your thoughts about your partner and relationship. You will examine them, observe them, and ask yourself if your emotions are real, or strong enough.

When it comes to ROCD symptoms, it often feels like your brain's stuck on a loop. You behave irrationally, and even if you are aware of it, you probably lack control and cannot stop. Keep in mind that this condition still requires a great deal of research, as specialists haven't yet unlocked everything there is to know about it. However, the risks for developing OCD can be found in family genes, or in your childhood development.

Some believe that OCD is something that is acquired through time; therefore, it cannot be unlearned. It is a physical problem with the functionality of the brain, except the exact source of the problem is difficult to find to start treating it properly. Behavioral therapists have had success in reducing symptoms of OCD and manage to influence their patients to take control of their lives once again.

When it comes to psychotherapy, many will agree that the source of ROCD lies in frequent thoughts of the relationship.

Thinking "What if he is not right for me?" is an ordinary thought that occurs to everyone. But if you keep returning to this thought, and over-analyze, this is referred to as habitual thinking. Your ideas count as experiences, and as you develop, your brain learns from experiences. Continually returning to this intrusive thought, you are teaching your brain, which can eventually lead to behavioral problems.

Treating ROCD

Many people combine cognitive behavioral therapy, mindfulness training, and anxiety management training to overcome obsessive-compulsive relationship disorder.

Cognitive behavioral therapy (CBT) will help with the obsessiveness you experience while having intrusive thoughts and it will also help you manage your compulsive behavior. CBT can aide you in achieving balance in your thought processes as it will teach you how to think rationally and how not to give in to the urge to repeat the same harmful behaviors that follow ROCD.

Mindfulness training can teach you how to let go of your harmful, obsessive thoughts. As mentioned earlier, the whole ROCD problem lies in intrusive thoughts, and you need to learn how to manage them properly and let them go.

However, anxiety management training is an essential part of overcoming ROCD. Learning how to manage the change in your behavior is playing a crucial role in the healing process. Treating ROCD is not easy, and it demands hard work and a great deal of thought and behavior change on your part. Keep in mind that this change might impact you negatively and even deepen your anxieties related to ROCD. In order for treatment to have the full effect, it is vital to learn how to deal with change.

CBT, mindfulness, and anxiety treatment give even better results when combined with" exposure with response prevention" treatment. The goal of ERP therapy is to expose the patient to situations or thoughts that trigger their ROCD and prevent them from reacting in the ways they are used to. In time, the patient will be able to face and successfully deal with the most feared situations that can trigger his ROCD.

If you notice any of the ROCD symptoms in you or a loved one, take it seriously. It is a condition that doesn't come easily to the one who is suffering, and it is nothing to be ashamed of. If your symptoms are severe, seek professional help, there are even approved medicines that help in the treatment of ROCD.

Chapter 6: Abandonment Anxiety Disorder

As the name suggests, relationship abandonment anxiety is the fear of being abandoned by your partner. It manifests itself through the constant need for attention and reassurance, due to your anxious behavior which is caused by the fear of abandonment. The source of abandonment anxiety is in the various attachment styles you develop as a child. To understand abandonment anxiety, you have to learn what your attachment style is and how to deal with it. In this chapter, we are going to focus on exploring this disorder and its effects on your relationship.

Attachment Styles

There are four main attachment styles that you can develop from your early childhood. As a baby, you are entirely dependent on your parents or caregivers for survival, food, primary care, love, etc. Therefore, you attach yourself to them as your primary source of safety. The ways people connect can vary because of the circumstances that are adapted. It can range from the cultural surroundings you are born in, to your caregiver's ability to provide for you.

We can say someone has a secure attachment style when he or she grows up in a supportive, loving environment. People with this kind of attachment have an easy time establishing a connection with others, and they provide emotional stability because they grew up in such a healthy environment.

However, an anxious-preoccupied attachment style develops when the caregiver responds poorly to his needs. These people develop low self-esteem issues and are unable to connect to others because of the constant worry of what others will think of them. They find themselves always comparing to others, and they have a very high opinion of everyone else but themselves.

A dismissive-avoidant attachment style usually develops in people deprived of an attachment figure. They learn to take care of themselves very early on and are unable to connect to others because they cannot allow themselves to depend on anyone. They have a high opinion of themselves and a lower one of others.

A fearful-avoidant attachment style is usually developed when you attach to a caregiver but suddenly find yourself deprived of that attachment figure due to various circumstances. This can be due to illness, death or any other kind of abandonment. It may also happen due to past traumatic experiences. For instance, if a child was a victim of any kind of abuse, he will develop a fearful-avoidant attachment style, and be afraid to connect to others out of the fear that the trauma will repeat itself. When a child feels deprived of love or care and is going through traumatic events such as divorce, the natural bond between him and the caregiver is disrupted. Depending on the individual child's coping mechanism, they might develop an anxious-avoidant attachment style.

Anxious-preoccupied and fearful-avoidant styles are the ones most often responsible for developing an abandonment anxiety disorder later in life when it comes to romantic relationships. People crave for attention, but they are also under the constant fear that the partner will abandon them.

The Effects of Separation Anxiety

Children feel anxious when they are separated from their caregivers because they do not grasp the concept of parents returning. They have no experience with being away from their parents, it is a new world to them, and they are afraid of it. It is only natural to feel this way, and it happens to all of us. Usually, when a child starts going to kindergarten and for the first time in his short life, he is separated from his parents for a longer time. Separation anxiety in children quickly passes as they are quite able to learn from experience that the parent will return and they will be reunited once again.

The problem can deepen if the child has issues adjusting to the new situation, and for some reason, he is unable to comprehend that his parents will return. In this case, the child's behavior will often change. Anxiety symptoms intensify and become excessive. Usually, a child is considered to be suffering from extreme separation anxiety if symptoms last longer than four weeks. And if the child is having a problem concentrating on school tasks and forming bonds with teachers or friends.

Separation anxiety can reappear later in life when you are an adult. It can be reflected on your relationship, and you may even experience the same symptoms once your partner needs to leave for a short time. The stress that separation anxiety puts on a relationship has the ability to destroy it, or at the very least damage it. If you are the one who suffers from it, you might put pressure on your partner to give you constant attention, reassurance, and to battle your fears. Your behaviors could drive the partner away from you, and the relationship will suffer. It is essential to have a coping mechanism in place if your partner needs to go somewhere without you. It may help to find love and support from another source other than your partner. Be open about your separation anxiety and work on it together. Be aware that your partner has his own life, and stress. You cannot put the burden of your anxiety on him and expect him to relieve all fears.

Abandonment Anxiety in Relationships

Although it stems from your childhood, abandonment anxiety can be projected on any romantic relationships you develop as an adult. When faced with the idea of losing a loved one, it can trigger your attachment style. Sometimes, people with abandonment issues will behave in ways that

66

they push their partners to leave them. This is one of the ways of coping with abandonment. Unconsciously, they speed up the process so their fear will be gone.

This behavior is unhelpful and deepens the fear, making it more intense and is placing the suffering person in a vicious cycle of anxiety. Once the fear is present, the person who suffers from abandonment anxiety will behave in such ways that affirm his fears, and he will never be able to get out of the loop. In order to be able to break away from this anxiety, you must understand your behaviors, why they appear, and how to change them. Some acts of abandonment anxiety are the following:

1. Sabotaging relationships, purposefully pushing the partner away, so you don't get hurt once he leaves you.

2. Having numerous shallow relationships. Mainly due to an inability to bond with your partner on a deeper level. When a partnership begins, the person suffering from abandonment anxiety will feel it's time to break up. The idea behind this behavior is that if you don't build a stable connection with your partner, it won't hurt once he leaves.

3. Clinging to bad relationships. Some people with abandonment anxiety might stay in unhealthy relationships at any cost because their fear of being alone is stronger than the need for security.

4. Need for constant reassurance. Need for your partner to affirm over and over again that he loves you and that he will never leave. Even with this continuous reassurance, you are still unable to trust them enough to gain relief from anxiety.

5. Separation anxiety. Believed only happens to children, it has been observed in adults too. Some people feel extreme anxiety symptoms when left alone, without a partner for short or long periods.

6. Panic is a common symptom of abandonment anxiety. When you don't hear from your partner for a set period of time, or he doesn't answer your calls, you might feel panic rising and demand to know what is going on immediately.

7. Fear of being alone. Spending every moment of the day in the same vicinity as your partner, in other words, being clingy, even having trouble sleeping without your partner being nearby.

In the long term, people with abandonment anxiety may develop other mental health issues, such as depression, mood swings, or even anger issues. These mental health problems may influence your future relationships, making potential partners feel alienated and force them to leave, thus restarting the cycle of abandonment.

Therapy

Therapy for abandonment anxiety can vary, and it mainly depends on the source of stress. For instance, we treat anxiety that has roots in abuse differently from those that stem from the death of a caregiver. However, most people who suffer from abandonment anxiety, manage to overcome their issues by combining more than one type of therapy. Here are some of the most common treatments used to combat abandonment anxiety:

1. Eye movement desensitization and reprocessing (EMDR) is used for treating trauma and can help people with abandonment anxiety if the root of it is in some past traumatic experience. It was first developed to treat PTSD but can also be used to treat any other type of trauma. EMDR is a type of therapy that will reprocess memories connected to the trauma and change your response to those memories.

2. Dialectical behavioral therapy (DBT) is one on one treatment with a professional, and it can teach you the skills needed to overcome

abandonment anxiety. Mindfulness and emotional regulation are one of these skills. It helps you learn how to talk to your partner and how to control your emotions and reactions.

3. Cognitive-behavioral therapy (CBT) will bring awareness to your past experiences that are causing your abandonment anxiety. By being aware of them, it will be easier for you to overcome them. It will help you set an objective view of your experiences and teach you how to differentiate the present situation from your past. This will also help disconnect any anxiety resulting from your past experiences and teach you how to behave in triggering situations.

4. Psychodynamic therapy can bring awareness to your attachment styles, and it can teach you about how you relate to others. You may learn how to change your bad habits which are related to the bonding process. It will also make you understand which defensive mechanisms you developed to cope with abandonment and it will attempt to improve them.

5. Couples therapy for abandonment anxiety. One or both partners may be dealing with abandonment anxiety. Couples therapy can help them deal with their issues, as well as relationship issues. It will also help them grow closer to each other and understand each other better.

6. Fear of abandonment couples therapy: This will help both partners understand each other better. If only one partner is suffering from fear of abandonment, the other one might not understand how past experiences can still influence his loved one. On the other hand, a partner that is suffering from anxiety will not understand how his loved one cannot put up with his behavior. His demand for attention and reassurance is not met. He doesn't see how that demand is negatively impacting his partner. Through couple's therapy, both partners will learn how to better interact with each other. They will learn how to express their needs in a healthy way

and communicate properly.

7. Emotional abandonment couples therapy: If you, or your partner, are dealing with abandonment anxiety that stems from a present situation. It could be manifesting itself through an emotional barrier between the two of you. Couples therapy may help you reconnect and find the system of bonding which suits both of you. A counselor can help you realize where the barrier is coming from, and help you explore your feelings to prepare you to be open again.

In addition to all the options above, you can attempt self-care for abandonment anxiety. It is essential that you learn how to take proper care of yourself if you are the one suffering from abandonment anxiety. To overcome this fear you must:

1. Learn to keep calm once the triggers overwhelm you. Find a safe space and attempt to objectify your fears.

2. Build your trust in others. Do not isolate yourself; instead, learn how to rely on others to better yourself.

3. Practice mindfulness. Pay attention to your thoughts and try to understand your fears, and ask yourself why do you feel this way, and where do your fears originate.

4. Learn how to communicate your needs. Instead of demanding attention and saying, "I need you to be there for me," say something like "I would feel safer if you would be there for me." Learn new communication skills; they will significantly reduce the number of misunderstandings you might have with your partner.

5. Acknowledge your past traumatic experiences. Don't ignore them, it will only affirm your fears, and it will not help your relationship.

Find the cause of your abandonment anxiety. Knowing the source will help you practice self-care with more ease. Your past abandonment experience happened, but you must realize it is not a pattern, and it will not necessarily happen again.

Helping your Partner

It is difficult to help someone who is suffering from abandonment issues, mostly because their reactions are unpredictable. If you bring up your concerns regarding their anxiety, they might lash out in anger and attack you, or they might completely withdraw within themselves and refuse to communicate. However, there are some things you can do to ease their anxiety and help them on their path to recovery:

1. Leave the conversation: If your partner becomes highly emotional, a conversation will be unhelpful. Both you and your partner might say things you don't mean to satisfy your needs. Step away from conversations like these, and let your partner know you care but do not give in to emotions. Instead, hold your partner, and show him with body language that you mean well, and return to having a conversation once emotions are less intense.

2. Don't respond to behavior triggered by anxiety: Your partner will demand attention by saying things like "I don't want to talk about it" or "leave me alone." If you continue to insist on a conversation, you will be trapped and unconsciously affirm his fears. Instead, take him for his word and don't respond. Let his emotions pass before engaging in a conversation.

3. Say how you feel: Be honest and tell him how his abandonment anxiety is influencing you, and how it is making you feel. He will realize it is not all about him and reconsider his actions to avoid hurting you.

All of the solutions listed above can help you understand how your abandonment anxiety came to be. You may learn its source and how to manage it, as such behaviors are influencing your relationship for the

71

worst. Therapy can teach you the skills you need to avoid or change those behaviors. With time and patience, this will lead to a happy and healthy relationship. Your insecurities and intrusive thoughts might return occasionally, and you might feel the need for more therapy, but don't get discouraged. Overcoming abandonment anxiety is a long process, and it requires devotion and self-care.

Chapter 7: Philophobia

Philophobia is the fear of love, the fear of falling in love, and the fear of committing and connecting to another person. The name of this phobia comes from the Greek word *Filos,* which means loving. You might think it is a somewhat unusual fear to have, but you would be surprised how often it occurs in people. As mentioned earlier phobias are anxiety disorders. They are irrational and extremely intense fears that can take control of you.

Most people have experienced bad relationships at some point and are hesitant to go into a new one after being hurt. This doesn't mean they all have philophobia. To characterize this fear as a phobia, present for over six months, produce irrational behavior and it is linked to other anxiety disorders.

Philophobia people do have emotions and feelings just like anyone else. They desire love, and to be showered in affection, but fear is making them incapable of any strong attachments. They will even consciously avoid making such connections to other people so they don't experience fear again. Philophobia leads to isolation and loneliness and has to be treated in order to achieve a healthy life.

The Cause

Some people are more prone to philophobia. People with experiences of drug and alcohol abuse, or depression, are more prone to develop any fear of attachment, including falling in love.

Causes for philophobia can vary from person to person. Everyone has his own story to tell. In this section we will take a look at some of the possible causes.

People who developed abandonment anxiety during childhood will often be afraid of love. For them, love means pain, so why would they fall in love? Abandonment anxiety develops when a child loses an important attachment figure. We attach to our parents because we need their support to survive. When we lose this support, we feel fear as a defensive mechanism that will keep us alive. When we lose a parent or both parents, whether they abandon us or pass away, we connect the love we felt for them with pain caused by their departure. For instance, many adopted children will even say how they were told things such as: "Your mother loved you so much she had to give you up because she couldn't care for you," or "You are so lucky, your mother loved you so much she would do anything for you – even give you up for your own benefit". Children who had experiences like this think that love equals abandonment. Therefore, they will avoid falling in love in the future, in order to avoid being abandoned again. They will even avoid marriage because commitment is too difficult when they expect to be abandoned.

In some cases, children are witnesses of toxic relationships filled with abuse among their parents. They connect romantic love to emotional turmoil because of their parent's behavior. They will develop a fear of being in love, and they will try to avoid reliving their parents' relationship.

When it comes to traumatic experiences from the past, they are not always connected to our childhood. Sometimes, a previous bad relationship will cause philophobia. It may come from being a victim of abuse, whether physical or verbal, and it might lead to a deep fear of bonding. To avoid possible damage, people who have philophobia will consciously decide not to give in to emotions and fall in love again.

Divorce can be another reason why people develop philophobia. Divorces are stressful, and if not managed with care, they can leave deep scars on our psyche. Separation can also mean abandonment, and it can affect us at any point in life. Divorce often means problems that we do not have control over. Losing control is an extremely uncomfortable feeling, which people try to avoid at all costs. Connecting it to a relationship can mean avoiding them altogether, so we always stay in control. Witnessing someone else's divorce, especially if it is painful for the one we care for, may lead to developing a fear of love. We won't allow ourselves to be in the same situation and will irrationally avoid relationships to avoid the same pain.

Cultural Norms

Love is a strong emotion, as it is a natural urge, and we want to give ourselves to it with our whole being. But in some cultures and religions, relationships can be seen as a sin. In these cases, we connect love with something bad, something we are not supposed to feel and experience. We will get punished if we give in to love. When it comes to a society that has developed such a concept of sinful love, punishment doesn't necessarily mean hurting the sinner. It is more about publicly shaming, making it known that a sin was committed. The sinners are made an example of and the belief that all relationships are bad is restored. Unfortunately, in some cultures, the punishment can go to extreme extents such as beatings, mutilation, and even death. Growing up in this environment can lead to the development of philophobia. It can deeply imprint on us. We will feel it even if we move into an open culture environment that does not regard love so harshly.

Uncertainty

Being in a relationship means sharing your life with someone. It means you will not always make the decisions, and you will not always be in control. This uncertainty is one of the things that make people fear relationships and avoid them. They are afraid of losing themselves within the relationship. They are usually looking only at the negative aspects of relationships and they fear them.

Painful experiences that we cannot avoid will eventually happen in any relationship. However, some try to dodge getting hurt in any way, and the uncertainty, or "what ifs," are common reasons why people develop philophobia. They often ask themselves what if they are forced to give more than they are willing to.

Depression

Depression seeks for loneliness and lowers our self-esteem. People with depression are aware of their illness, and they fear more than getting hurt. They fear that they will harm their loved ones and make them suffer because of their pain. They are aware of depression influencing the whole relationship and quality of life for both partners. This is why they are prone to develop a fear of making connections with people. They fear that their depression will bring suffering to others.

People who suffer from depression feel hopeless. They are unable to see the future of their relationship and think life may never get better. Putting this distorted view of being on your partner's shoulders can be overwhelming for both of you. Even everyday relationship problems, to a depressed person, may seem impossible to solve. They will stop trying because in their minds there is no hope. They cannot invest anything in a relationship, and they are avoiding it to such an extent that they develop philophobia.

Symptoms

Philophobia can cause extreme reactions when facing the object of fear; in this case, not just love; it is the possibility of love. We experience the symptoms of philophobia when we are in the company of a person we are attracted to. Because we see this person as our potential partner, just looking at him or her may trigger our phobia. The symptoms of any phobia might strike you as scary because they come in an uncontrollable wave of intensity, and they affect us, not just emotionally, but physically too. The most common symptoms and characteristics are:

1. Extreme nervousness when we are around a possible love interest.

2. Suppressing our emotions and the thoughts we have towards a love interest.

3. Avoiding places and situations that will lead to being reminded of love, such as meeting with our love interest, or avoiding places where couples go.

4. Avoiding friends and family's marriage ceremonies.

5. Complete isolation from the outside world, retreating yourself from society.

6. Racing heart rate when we see the love interest, excessive shaking, breathing troubles, sweating, nausea, and even fainting.

All of these symptoms can manifest themselves even when you love interest is not around or doesn't even exist yet. Some people affected with philophobia will display signs even when they just themselves in any situation that reminds them of love or a relationship. Some of them will often make excuses and convince themselves why they do not need companionship. However, due to social norms, they are unable to recognize the phobia in themselves, and they think in the following way:

1. I'm too busy for a relationship. I do not have the time or energy for it.

2. Love is too much work, and I cannot devote myself at the moment.

3. I can't find the one who fits my description of the perfect partner.

4. Who needs love? My life rocks just the way it is.

5. I love the freedom I have.

6. I don't want to be suffocated by a relationship.

7. I don't like all the drama that accompanies a relationship.

8. I love the simple life, without romantic complications.

Most of the time, these are just excuses and lies, and people can usually see right through them. They are not there to convince anyone. They make a philophobic person feel better about themselves by finding a way to cope with his or her issues. If you notice that you're making these excuses for yourself frequently, it may be the time to seek someone's guidance.

Treatment

Society doesn't see philophobia as a threat and will often joke about it because it sounds silly. While it is a strange phobia, it is as serious as any other phobia. It can have a severe impact on anyone's life, and it can prevent people from living their lives to their fullest. A philophobic person often leads an isolated life, never knowing the benefits of a healthy relationship. Some are usually in constant distress, and their fear of love will influence their everyday life. They often struggle with common tasks and feel incredibly lonely at the same time.

Philophobia can be treated with psychotherapy and medication, so you don't have to suffer from it your entire life. However, medication is only given to patients with extreme philophobia, and most cases psychotherapy is enough.

For instance, Cognitive behavioral therapy (CBT) may help you recognize the thoughts that trigger philophobia and manage them properly. A therapist will talk to a person who has philophobia and helps him change his beliefs about love and relationships. Building a positive behavior as a response to the triggering thoughts is another benefit of CBT.

Exposure therapy is another option. It relies on setting the scene that usually triggers the anxiety associated with philophobia, through controlled exposure to objects and situations that hold the meaning of love for the afflicted person. This may include simulating dates, watching romantic movies, and even encouraging interaction with a possible love interest. The therapist observes how these situations affect the patient and how he or she reacts to them. The goal of exposure therapy is to build enough experience to reduce and control the anxiety that follows philophobia.

Keep in mind that phobias are not common fears and do not attempt to treat own philophobia. It may help you and bring temporary relief, but most often, it will only bury your true feelings towards love deeper inside. Do not be afraid to seek outside help if you think you have philophobia. It is nothing to be ashamed of there are therapists and doctors that understand how severely it can affect your life and try their best to help you.

Chapter 8: How to Live a Happy Relationship

Relationships require maintenance and constant work for it to succeed and turn into a long, loving, and happy relationship. People are often taught that love just happens, and sometimes they are even told that for a relationship to be successful, love is all that is needed. However, relationships are much more than that and love is not enough. Love can be the first spark that ignites the relationship and is how it came to exist. To build a long-lasting connection with another person, you need to think in more realistic terms when it comes to defining love. Expanding on the simplistic view, or fairytale, you dreamt of when you were young is the first step.

For a happy relationship, you have to actively work on it and make the best of everything you encounter on your path to happiness. Having a happy relationship means making conscious choices that will work towards that happiness, even if sometimes the decisions you make seem difficult and challenging.

Everyone makes mistakes when it comes to relationships, and we aren't referring to solely romantic ones. Even with friends, our behavior might influence how much they trust us, rely on us, and how much we will connect with them, and on what level. The fact we all make mistakes doesn't mean there is nothing you can do about it. There is actually a lot! There are actions both you and your partner can take to avoid mistakes, manage them if they already happened, and bring happiness to your relationship:

1. Your partner is your equal: This is something people often forget when they are bossing each other around. Do you recognize yourself or your partner while reading this? Instead of being the leader of the relationship, try collaboration. Work together, listen to your partner, and be as supportive as possible.

2. Be respectful: Spending a lot of time with one person can be indeed

exhausting, especially if you live with your partner. Sometimes, it may seem like your partner is triggering your nerves or anxiety, and you may feel anger or resentment building up. You may end up lashing out even if he or she isn't entirely at fault. No matter how you feel, how angry you are, your partner needs to learn about such emotions respectively. Communication plays an important role here as well as self-control. Practice both of these even outside of your relationship, and you will see only the positive influence it leaves on people.

3. Spend quality time with your partner: Back when your relationship was fresh and new, you spent so much time together, and you did everything together. Where did all of that go? Well, life happens, children come, people focus on their jobs and careers, home, chores, and so on. Some may lose all of their free time that they used to devote to their partners. Even so, for a relationship to succeed, you need to make that time even when it's scarce. Happy relationships demand you to push yourself and your partner and do something together. It is not enough to talk to each other at the end of the day about work or various problems. Quality time means getting to work together on a project. For instance, you can repaint your home, build a dollhouse for your kids, go hiking or exercising together, volunteer in an animal shelter, and so on. By working together on something that you are both interested in, you will reconnect and even learn new things about each other. It is a satisfying and enriching experience.

4. Learn how to forgive: It is essential to know how to forgive your partner's mistakes, but you also have to be willing to forgive yourself. Empathy plays a significant role in forgiveness. It helps you feel your partner's emotions, understand their behavior, and make room in your heart for real and unconditional forgiveness. Be the same towards yourself. Learn self-compassion and practice it. It is a great skill that will not just heal wounds created by mistakes, but also teach you not to repeat them.

5. Expectations: When you commit to someone, it doesn't mean you are supposed to rely on him or her to make you happy. Young couples often make this mistake. Your partner is your companion through life and not just an accessory. Do not expect your partner to completely understand you or know you as this can rarely be achieved by anyone and it will only cause you various feelings of anxiety. Remember that you are two individuals with your own experiences and you are supposed to complement each other. He is not entirely responsible for your happiness. Just being with your partner should bring you relief and joy, and if you want more from your relationship, it is up to you to make it happen. If there is something your partner could do and it would make you happy, be open about it, and say it clearly. People cannot read minds and relationships often fail simply due to the lack of communication, which stems from having unclear expectations and making assumptions.

Confidence, Honesty and Loyalty

The three most desirable traits people seek in their love interests are confidence, honesty, and loyalty. But they do not come naturally to everyone. Some gain them during their childhood, while others have to learn them and stay true to them to build a healthy, stable relationship.

Confidence

We quickly develop low self-esteem if you are hurt in a previous relationship. It may be difficult to win back your trust, but it is not impossible. Confidence should be strong yet yielding, as overconfident people can be inflexible and bad listeners. However, the right amount will improve your relationship, the way you react in stressful situations, and it will positively affect your health. There is a series of exercises you could do everyday to build your confidence, such as the following:

1. Have a clear picture of what you want to be: Visualizing your goals is a fantastic technique to build motivation. It will keep you going and remind you of your aspirations and goals. Don't be afraid to talk about what you want with friends, family, and especially with your partner. They can help you get there, with proper advice or with support.

2. Affirm yourself: It means you need to vocalize positive statements and opinions regarding yourself. It may sound silly at first, but hearing it, even hearing yourself saying it out loud, will help you believe it. The human brain tends to accept statements more quickly if they are in the form of a question. Instead of saying, "I am good with money," try asking yourself, "why am I so good with money?"

3. Challenge yourself: Once a day, do something that scares you. In most cases, the best way to overcome fear is to face it. Anxieties often stop people from performing simple, everyday tasks like making a phone call, going to the bank, or meeting new people. Doing things that scare you will push you to realize that you can improve yourself. Going through the challenge may even boost your self-confidence and in time help you get over some of your anxieties. Just be sure to make a ritual of it and challenge yourself every day.

4. Approve of yourself: People with various anxieties will often criticize themselves due to the impossible standards they have in place. However, this behavior usually leads to a great deal of anxiety and strain on a relationship. Instead of listening to your inner critic, try approving of yourself instead. Give yourself a pat on the back for a job well done, instead of overthinking whether

you performed well enough. Offering yourself this approval is not easy, especially if you're low on self-esteem. If you find this to be a difficult step, you can try the following exercise: is your inner voice telling you how you are a failure? Ask yourself what evidence is there to support the thought that you are indeed a failure? Now ask yourself, is there evidence that proves you are not a failure? Write everything down, go over your lists and focus on the positive rather than negative. It's enough for just a small dose of positive thinking to outweigh and overwhelm the negative thoughts.

5. Start small: Many people fail because their goals are too challenging. Some people are perfectionists, and any small error will be considered a failure. If you find yourself in this situation, you need to take your time and set small goals that are easy to accomplish. These small goals will build a stream of success that boosts confidence, and you will feel ready for larger ones because now you know you can reach them. Remind yourself of your daily accomplishments, as they will keep you motivated and confident enough to accomplish anything you set out to achieve.

Honesty

Being honest is so much more than telling the truth. It also means not keeping any secrets from your partner, caring for others, and having integrity. Being honest means your partner can fully rely on you, trust you with his whole heart, and be proud of you. Take note, that even small "white" lies can generate relationship problems, mistrust, and anxiety, for yourself as well as your partner once he or she learns the truth. If you find yourself telling small lies due to your stress, you may need to practice honesty. Here are the steps you can take to learn how to be completely honest without being anxious:

1. Understand why you lied: Did you fabricate things to make

84

yourself look better? Or to avoid embarrassment? Understanding why you lied is a big step forward to changing the things about you for the better. People lie for various reasons but being aware of those reasons will help you deal with them in other ways. Maybe you need to work on your confidence, or you think you deserve more respect. Try to earn it with honesty instead of making up stories about yourself. People often lie out of shame or out of a lack of confidence and self-esteem. For instance, if you did something you aren't proud of, you may be tempted to cover it up with lies. Many people even lie to themselves in an attempt to get rid of that feeling of shame. Instead, be responsible and accept your bad behavior because acceptance allows you to take the steps needed to correct it. This way, you will show others that you can be honest and possibly someone to trust and rely on.

2. Change your behavior: Guilt is a powerful feeling, and any behavior that has led you to experience it will cause anxiety. When you are found guilty by others, you may also lose their respect. Being guilty and admitting it will more often bring understanding instead of judgment, especially when it comes to your partner who loves you. However, you should not rely on knowledge alone. Try to change bad habits and behaviors and avoid putting yourself in a situation that will make you feel guilty and that will make you lie to your loved ones.

3. Don't compare yourself to others: In our attempt to be better and earn respect, we often lie about who we are. You need to accept who you are and to learn to live with it, even if you see yourself in a negative light. Don't forget that anxiety often makes people overly critical of themselves, and you might not be as faulty as you think. Improve yourself, work on your personality, and become who you want to be instead of lying about it. Instead of making up things about yourself to impress your partner, let your honesty impress him. It will build a connection between the two of you, and it will make your relationship stronger.

4. Avoid lying for others: Sometimes, our friends and family will put us in stressful situations and ask us to lie for them. Let them know this is not an option for you and that you are an honest person. If they want you to keep a secret for them, be sure you can do it, and don't give in to the temptation of gossip.

Loyalty

When we think about loyalty in a relationship, it usually means as not cheating. But, loyalty also implies devotion to your partner, being faithful, committed, and honest. Loyalty is so much more than just fidelity. It means opening yourself to your partner and sharing all of your emotions, thoughts, and opinions. Here's what you can do to show and prove your loyalty to your partner:

1. If you want to be truly loyal to your partner, you have to be honest with yourself. Practice transparency, get to know yourself and be aware of who you are. We often have the wrong image of ourselves, and if you don't know yourself, how could you offer to be connected to someone else. How can you share yourself, and commit?

2. Be open with your partner. Not just honest but let them read you. Share your emotions and opinions at the end of your day. Sit down with your partner and spend time talking about your day. Include all the events and express how it made you feel and how it has influenced you.

3. Don't put yourself in the position that will make you hide something from your partner. Don't hide events, experiences, and don't hide your emotions. Keeping secrets is postponing the inevitable. Secrets always come out one way or another and your attempt to hide them will just cause pain for you and your partner.

4. Be supportive. Be there for your partner through the good and bad. We all have our moments when even the slightest tantrum will trigger anxiety. Don't judge your partner. Don't tell him or her how to behave or what to do. Support them with understanding and care. Don't say things like "There is no reason to be angry", say it "I understand why would that make you angry".

Improving Communication

Communication is the key ingredient to a happy relationship. Without it, there will be a lot of misunderstandings, unclear emotions, or thoughts that will never be vocalized. If you learn how to communicate with your partner properly, you will avoid unpleasant situations. Keep in mind that communication has to be nonviolent and free of judgment. Approaching issues in a relationship with an open mind is what will improve the quality of your relationship. Sometimes it is difficult to control the things we are saying, especially if we are angry, sad, or annoyed. But with practice, you can gain control, and you can learn how to achieve a positive outcome in any conversation you have with your partner.

Let's say you are at a restaurant, waiting for your partner who is late. You feel annoyed at first having to sit alone while you wait. After some time the feeling develops into frustration and anger. Once your partner finally shows up, you don't wait to hear excuses, you lash out. This is your anxiety taking control. Try to recognize why you lash out and regain control. Don't assume why your partner is late, that will feed into your insecurities. Instead, ask calmly what happened to make him so late. Let them know you felt uncomfortable sitting alone, and you would like them to realize that next time, and maybe they should call. This is an effective way of informing your partner know that you are bothered by the behavior, and you will avoid an unpleasant argument. Your agitation will be much shorter, and you will be able to enjoy your dinner date.

The way you respond to a partner's communication attempt is also important. Be sure to get acquainted with the *appreciative feedback* technique. It is a communication technique that offers support. It inspires your partner to be more open, and both of you will stay focused on the positive outcome of the situation. For example, if your partner comes from work and informs you that an important meeting earlier that day went well, you could respond with appreciative feedback and say "That is great! I am so happy for you. Tell me more about it". Share the enthusiasm with your partner and show genuine interest in whatever he has to say. Asking questions will make your partner relive that good experience, boosting his confidence and motivate him to continue. It will show how much you care about things in his life, and how happy it makes you to see him this positive.

You should value your partner and show it to him by appropriately talking to him. Do not be cold and distant, and don't ignore what he has to say. Do not interrupt him, and never change the subject if he is not finished talking. Communication in a romantic relationship can go beyond words as every gesture you make can show respect and interest. Be mindful of what your partner likes and dislikes and show how much you care with just the right amount of intimacy. Body language and facial expressions are important for non-verbal communication skills. Don't be afraid to show how you feel by using them, as you will place an accent on your excitement and thus encourage your partner to respond. For instance, you can frown in disagreement instead of putting it into words, as this signal is enough to display your feelings and your partner will understand your intentions. Let your face show your emotions, you do not have to openly say how you feel. Humans are good at reading faces. It is how we know when someone is lying to us, the same way we know when someone is looking at us with love.

Communication is a skill that is learned. Take any chance you have to practice with your family, friends, or colleagues. Remember that words are the result of our emotions and thoughts. They can hurt, so be mindful of what you are saying and to whom you are saying it. Be sure your intuition can predict how your partner will respond to your communication attempt. Also, learn how to listen; it is an even better skill than talking. Try to listen without being distracted by surrounding "noise," focus on your partner instead. Show empathy and validation, be quick to encourage him, but never judge. Proper communication will improve your relationship, and it will be a clear sign of how much you appreciate your partner.

Chapter 9: Techniques for Anxiety Reduction

To reduce symptoms of anxiety there are exercises you and your partner can do. If you are not the one who suffers from anxiety, it is imperative to be a support to your partner. Join him or her in performing these exercises. You might even be surprised how beneficial they can be for the reduction of overall stress.

The exercises are simple, anyone can do them, and they work best if they are combined. Don't choose just one, try them all and see what suits you best. Some should be done every day, others on occasion. But they will have the best result if you find your tempo, get used to the new routine, and enjoy them with your significant other.

Distract yourself

This exercise is simple, and it doesn't give away the feeling of a task. However, it is difficult to practice it while you are in the middle of an anxiety attack, so keep that in mind. Sometimes you will lack focus, and other times you won't find these activities as pleasurable. This is why you should have your partner helping you and joining you whenever it is possible. Here are some of the activities you could do together:

1. Watch a comedy movie or comedy stand up show.

2. Exercise together or go for a hike.

3. Clean the house together or work on renovating a room.

4. Try out a new restaurant.

5. Play your favorite game together.

Alternatively, you can come up with your pleasurable activities. The idea is to distract yourself from all of your worries and anxieties with something that gives you pleasure. The above are just examples, and you do not need to follow them. Make a list. The time will eventually come when it will be difficult to think of an activity you could use to distract yourself from your anxiety. Make a second list of activities you could do on your own, in case your partner is not with you at that time. Try crocheting, painting, volunteering, walking a dog, etc.

Mindful Breathing

This exercise will help you practice focusing on the present moment, and it will help you concentrate. Mindful breathing refers to counting your breaths while being aware of each one of them. Breathing is a reflex that nobody thinks about. Breath is life; without it, we wouldn't survive. Bring your breathing to a level of awareness by following a few simple steps:

1. Sit or lie down comfortably in a room that feels safe.

2. Focus on your breathing, try to discern whether you breathe with your chest or abdomen.

3. Do not try to control your breathing. It has to be natural. Don't control its pace or how much air you take in. This exercise can be challenging as awareness of your breathing often results in an attempt to control it. For now, you need to fight this urge and let it be natural.

4. Keep yourself focused on breathing, your mind may wander, but you have to remind yourself why you are doing this exercise and return your focus to breathing.

5. Finish your mindful breathing in a set time frame. You can set an alarm to remind you the time is up. Stretch your body and notice

how you feel. What are your emotions, and are there any intrusive thoughts? Keep in mind that the point of this exercise is awareness, it doesn't matter what you are thinking or feeling.

Keep in mind that you will have bad days and good days, so try to practice mindful breathing as often as you can. Start with a five minutes exercise and slowly progress to 10, 20 and 30 minutes. Usually, there is no need for more than that.

Abdominal Breathing

The way an anxious person breathes is fundamental. During an anxiety attack, your breath becomes shallow and comes from your chest. This type of breathing can intensify your symptoms of anxiety. Shallow, chest breathing can also cause hyperventilation, which is similar to a panic attack and will cause even more instability in a person with an anxiety disorder. Because of this, it is very important to practice abdominal breathing.

Abdominal breathing will raise the levels of oxygen in your brain and muscles, and it will stimulate the parasympathetic nervous system, which is responsible for calming you down. The benefits of abdominal breathing can be enormous for people suffering from any anxiety disorder as well as panic attacks. You could ask your partner to join you in practicing this breathing as it can benefit anyone. Here is how to do it properly:

1. Sit or lie comfortably. Place one hand on your chest, and the other on your abdomen. Breathe naturally without attempting to control it. Notice which hand is rising while you are inhaling.

2. Control your next breath and try to make it as deep as possible so that it moves the hand which lies on your abdomen. Inhale through your nose slowly while counting to four.

3. When you are done inhaling make a pause and count to four once again, while holding your breath.

4. Exhale slowly to a count of five. You can exhale through your nose or mouth, it doesn't matter, as long as you feel comfortable.

5. After you completely emptied your lungs, take two normal, natural breaths without controlling them.

6. Repeat each step and continue this cycle for five minutes.

Abdominal breathing exercises should be practiced on a daily basis. It will calm you down and teach you how to focus. Keep in mind that it is extremely helpful in crisis situations when a panic attack is possible. It will calm you immediately and take the focus from intrusive thoughts to calm breathing.

Visualization

Even professional athletes use the technique of visualization to prepare themselves for competitions. They visualize themselves crossing the finish line and see the personal record time they set for themselves. Visualization is an excellent way to relax and reduce stress. It will allow you to mentally remove yourself from anxious behaviors without effort to overcome them. Visualization will help you turn off intrusive thoughts that cause anxiety and will help you focus on the task ahead. Visualize using your sense of smell, hearing and touch by following these steps:

1. Relax comfortably somewhere where you won't be interrupted. Devote at least 20 minutes for this exercise. Close your eyes and breathe abdominally for 2 minutes.

2. Imagine a place that feels safe to you. It can be a real place where

you were always welcome and where you felt calm, such as your grandparent's home, a meadow, beaches, forests, etc.

3. Imagine yourself being in this perfectly calming place. It is in your head, and you can go there whenever you feel like.

4. If you are visualizing a familiar place that always felt safe, try to remember the smell of that place. If it is a new one, an imagined place where you never went before, try to feel the smell of a familiar flower, damp earth, ocean breeze or sun lotion.

5. Imagine the sounds of that place. It can be birds singing, ocean waves crashing, or a familiar calming song playing on the radio.

6. Try to imagine the sun warming you up, the wind blowing on your skin, or the touch of grass on your bare feet.

7. Engage your mind in exploring the place. See where you are. Are there clouds in the sky? What colors do you see? Is the light bright or dim, are there any shadows?

8. Once you feel completely relaxed, open your eyes and slowly become aware of your real surroundings. Remember, whenever you feel the need, you can always go to your safe place in your mind and calm yourself down.

All of these techniques for anxiety reduction can be practiced alone, however for some of them you may want to engage your partner as your external support. Any of these methods will help you reduce anxiety temporarily but they will also have long term effects by teaching you how to focus and calm down. Combined with therapy and self-care, techniques for anxiety reduction will help you battle your fears and build a strong, healthy relationship with your partner.

Chapter 10: Loving a Person with Anxiety

This final chapter is dedicated to partners of people who struggle with anxiety. Relationship and love demands that we get involved in our partner's life and this means we always have to be supportive and loving. If you have a partner with one or more types of anxiety, you are already aware of how it can influence not just the relationship, but your life too. Anxiety comes in many forms, and there is no magic pill that can help. Anxiety is also an individual experience that can differ in many ways. The list of things we can do to help our partner when they are having an anxiety attack differs from person to person. You should know how to recognize the symptoms and learn how to neutralize an anxiety attack by relying on previous experience.

Your involvement in your partner's journey of learning how to live a life free of anxiety is of great importance. When it comes to sudden panic attacks, you can do several different things to help distract your partner and ease any suffering. When it comes to chronic anxiety, you are the one who will get involved in exposure therapy. There are specific strategies you can take into consideration when it comes to each type of anxiety. This chapter will help you recognize which type of stress your partner is struggling with and learn how to help him. You will be able to improve the quality of your relationships, strengthen the bond you have, and confirm your love and devotion to your partner.

Acute Anxiety

Acute anxiety happens out of the blue. It can be caused by different things, certain situations or other people you and your partner meet. It happens suddenly, and there is no time for planning and taking it slow. You need to be able to react in the moment and to know how to assess the situation.

Understand what is happening, what your partner is going through, and come up with the right way that can help neutralize the anxiety. There are four steps you can take to be supportive and helpful in case of acute anxiety:

1. Be calm, be compassionate. If you are not, you won't be able to support your partner needs at that moment. If you give in to anger, frustration, or your own anxiety, it won't help. It can even make things worse. You also need to remember not to give in to your partner's anxiety and accommodate it. In the long run, this is not helpful. Instead, offer understanding, not just solutions.

2. Assess your partner's anxiety. What level is it? What are the symptoms and signs of an anxiety attack? An anxiety attack can hit with a different strength each time. You need to be able to recognize it to choose actions appropriate to the given situation.

3. Remind your partner of the techniques that helped with previous anxiety attacks. Whether it is breathing or exercise, your partner is probably aware of their success in neutralizing anxiety. But in the given situation, maybe he or she needs reminding. Once they are on the right path of dealing with anxiety, your job is to provide positive reinforcement. Give praise and be empathetic once your partner executes techniques that will help with an anxiety attack.

4. Evaluate the situation. Is your partner's anxiety attack passing? If it is, be supportive and encourage your partner to continue whatever he is doing to lower his anxiety. If it stays at the same level, or increases, you should start the steps from the beginning and come up with different techniques and strategies to help your partner with an acute anxiety attack.

Chronic Anxiety

To address chronic anxiety, you might have to try out exposure therapy, as it is considered the golden standard of treatment by many people. Usually, it takes the guidance of a professional therapist to try with exposure therapy. But, if the level of your partner's anxiety is not severe, you might feel comfortable enough to try it on your own. In this case, you have to act as a guide and learn how to be a supportive person for your partner.

Exposure therapy works by creating situations that trigger your partner's anxiety. This will help your partner learn how he or she can tolerate certain levels of anxiety. Your partner will learn how to reduce anxiety and how to manage it in given situations. Over time, you might get surprised how your partner learned to enjoy situations that previously made them anxious.

You have to start with the least challenging situation and progress slowly and steadily towards more challenging ones. Don't push your partner to the next level until they are ready. If anxiety isn't decreasing in the first challenge, it's not time to go to second. If a situation is causing too much anxiety, and your partner feels he or she is not ready to deal with it, go back to previous challenge and work on it again.

For example, let's say your partner has a fear of heights. He or she wants to overcome this fear and be able to climb the buildings last floor. How will exposure therapy look in this case?

1. Tell your partner to look out the window from the ground floor for exactly one minute.

2. Climb to the second floor together with your partner. Remember that you are not just an exposure therapy guide; you also need to act as a support. Make them look out the window from the second floor for one minute. In case of anxiety showing up in its first

97

symptoms, remind your partner to do breathing exercises to lower its impact.

3. Once your partner feels better, they should try looking out the window again.

4. If no anxiety presents itself, you should leave your partner's side. They need to be able to look through the same window, but this time without you.

5. Climb to the third floor and repeat steps three and four. When your partner feels ready, continue to the fourth floor, sixth and so on. If your partner's anxiety is too high, don't hesitate to stop. The first session doesn't need to take longer than 30 minutes.

6. Each new session needs to begin with the last comfortable floor your partner experienced. You don't need to always start from the ground floor, as your partner progresses, feeling no anxiety when looking through the window of the second, third, even fourth floor.

7. Take time. Your partner will not be free of the fear in just a few days. Be patient and continue practicing exposure therapy in this way until your partner can achieve the goal and climb the last floor.

8. The goal of exposure therapy is not just to get rid of fear and anxiety. It should also teach your partner that he or she can control and tolerate discomfort. Your partner will have an opportunity to practice anxiety-reduction techniques in a safe and controlled environment, with you in the support role.

Specific Disorder Interventions

If you have a partner who has been diagnosed with a particular anxiety disorder, you can try the techniques described in this section. Under the guidance of a trained therapist, the two of you will learn how to approach it in the best possible way. Your partner's therapist might ask you to join in a few sessions, and he will teach you how to better help your partner in situations that elevate anxiety. If your partner is not diagnosed, but both of you suspect he might have a certain disorder, advise your partner to visit a doctor. Self-diagnosing can lead to mistakes, and you will make wrong choices in how to approach your partner's anxiety.

Panic Disorder with Agoraphobia

If this is your partner's diagnosis, you two probably already have a pattern of behavior that is designed to accommodate your partner's anxiety. You probably follow your partner to social events, and you are the one who is in charge of running errands outside of the house. This accommodation is counterproductive in the long run. You are showing that you care, love, and support your partner, but it prevents him or her from experiencing a full life. Your partner needs to learn how to overcome anxiety. You may approach panic disorder with exposure therapy, so your partner becomes less dependent on you:

1. Choose an errand that your partner thinks he can handle himself. It can be shopping, going to a doctor appointment alone, walking a dog, etc.

2. Plan what errands are more challenging for your partner and add them to the list. Write them down as "to be accomplished in the future." It is important to work slowly but keep a clear vision of what needs to be accomplished.

3. Work together on slowly accomplishing the first task on your list. If it's going shopping alone, accompany your partner a few times, so they are accustomed to the environment. When he or she feels confident enough to go alone, let them. Encourage and support their decision.

4. Once your partner accomplishes the task, be there to discuss his experience about it. Listen carefully and address any issues that might arise. Encourage your partner and keep track of his progress.

Obsessive-Compulsive Disorder

When it comes to OCD, what you can do for your partner is not to engage in his behaviors. Also, encourage him not to give in and repeat their compulsive behaviors. If you give in and comply with your partner's OCD, you will not be helping. Although it will surely elevate the tension made by your partner's OCD, complying will reinforce the fears. For example, if your partner asks you to go to the kitchen and make sure all appliances are off, you shouldn't comply. But you should also not argue or call your partner irrational. It is ineffective, and it will only deepen the anxiety.

What you could do to help him overcome OCD is to use communication skills you learned in previous chapters. Discuss with your partner how is it best to approach anxiety and agree on a strategy. This is where a professional therapist will be of most use to both of you. A professional can guide you through this conversation and help both of you feel comfortable discussing the delicate topic of your partner's disorder.

You will need to learn how to change from saying things like:

"I will not go to the kitchen again, you are imagining things, and being irrational" to "I appreciate your concern about the kitchen appliances, but we agreed that the best thing we can do is to help you learn how to manage the feelings you are having right now."

Your partner will agree for their own benefit that the best thing you could do is stay by their side, not check the kitchen, and help them work through the anxiety. This can be done with breathing exercises that will help your partner calm down. In time, your partner will show less fear. The OCD will decrease, and you will feel less frustrated.

Generalized Anxiety Disorder

The behavior of people with GAD is similar to that of people who have OCD. They have fears about certain things, and these fears are not comforted by reassurance. GAD usually creates concerns that we all have. It can be about finances, health, and school. But people with GAD will overblow the proportion of these fears, and they will influence their daily life. If your partner is diagnosed with GAD, you are aware of how simple problems we face everyday can sound like total catastrophes. Your partner probably assumes the worst possible end of certain situations.

People will GAD often express physical discomforts such as headaches, stomach pains, or muscle soreness. This can influence your intimate life and add up to the anxiety. When one partner suffers from GAD, the other usually joins in for a couple's therapy. This is because GAD is constantly creating underlying problems in the relationship that need to be dealt with. A therapist can educate a couple about GAD and examine what is causing the anxiety. GAD can be developed because one of the partners feels they are not allowed to make major decisions. He or she may feel like his partner is neglecting their opinion.

It often happens that people with this affliction develop a constant feeling of inadequacy. They believe they are not good enough for their partners, and that they never will be. When this happens, they usually try to overcompensate and make everything perfect so their partner can love them. On the other hand, some may feel that there is nothing they can do and that there is no point in trying. They underperform reinforcing their feelings of inadequacy.

If your partner suffers from GAD, the best way to help is to join the therapy session and discover the underlying problems that are occurring in your relationship. Learn how to deal with them. It can be anything from money concerns, to sexual dissatisfaction, or just communication problems. A therapist will teach you both techniques that will help you and your partner change the way of thinking. This involves recognizing the thoughts that cause anxiety. Once identified, you will have to challenge those thoughts and assess the likelihood of anxiety-provoking events even happening. Help your partner practice alternative thoughts and listen to the therapist's advice on how else you can influence your partner's GAD.

Social Phobia

Social phobia comes in many forms. It can make going to work a very difficult task, or it can make maintaining relationships impossible to achieve. A therapist uses the technique of testing the hypothesis of a patient. They will ask the patient to perform a task that makes them anxious, and later, they will analyze what happened. This is a very successful way of bringing realization to the patient that their fears and anxieties do not have a foundation. A therapist can teach a person with social phobia the basic communication skills to prepare them for situations they might encounter in their endeavors to overcome anxiety.

You can also practice this technique with your partner. Encourage them to test the hypothesis. Instead of avoiding social situations, encourage them to participate. If he or she is afraid of going to parties because they might be rejected by people, encourage to go, and tag a long to be supportive. Once at the party, encourage them to approach people and start conversations. Practice easy starter lines beforehand and let them decide when or who to talk to. They should know how to interpret social behaviors in the right way. Encourage your partner to gather information about experiences to take to the therapist for further analysis. It is all part of the journey to overcome his phobia.

You can also help by planning with your partner how to cope with situations that will trigger his anxiety. You may not always be present when he needs to gather experience. Make a plan for how to react in situations where your partner is facing anxiety triggering events alone and encourage them to try it. Challenge your partner's thoughts about failure and help determine if the fears are valid. Empathize with your partner and validate those feelings. Help them interpret events that caused the anxiety and put it in a different light. In time, social events might even become a newly discovered pleasure for your partner.

Post-Traumatic Stress Disorder

PTSD is caused by experiencing a traumatic event, and it can affect every aspect of a relationship. If your partner is suffering from PTSD he or she will react to certain triggers that will remind him of the traumatic experience. In the case of PTSD, anxiety attacks can happen both spontaneously and routinely. Often people who have PTSD become disconnected from their partners when anxiety hits them. They become unresponsive to their partners, or they don't even recognize them for what they are.

When remembering a traumatic event, your partner's behavior might become unpredictable and frightening. You might even find yourself in danger and fear for your safety. This is why PTSD requires special attention.

You should remember that your partner's behavior during a PTSD attack is not the one that reflects his true feelings about you. Don't take actions that might provoke your partners PTSD. Don't drive past the place where the attack happened, or don't watch movies with vivid war scenes.

PTSD requires professional help for your partner to become less sensitive to triggering situations. You need to support and encourage your partner on his way to recovery. Be patient and listen to your partner. Validate his feelings and create an environment where both of you will feel safe.

Make a Plan for Relieving your Partner's Anxiety

Now you know potential techniques you can use to reduce your partner's anxiety. Use this knowledge to create a plan, make a list of practical actions and ineffective actions for when your partner experiences anxiety attack. It is important to remember what to do in situations that trigger anxiety, but it is also important to know what not to do.

You and your partner might disagree with what is helpful on the list you are making. This is because your partner craves for accommodative behaviors you express when they are under an anxiety attack. Remember that these behaviors relieve the anxiety, but in the long run, they do more damage. Try to explain this to your partner. You need to make them understand why such behavior is not suitable for anyone.

Teamwork is beneficial when it comes to fighting partner's anxiety. But your partner might not want your help due to feelings of shame, or they think they don't need help. Try making a list on your own. It's worthwhile to do what you can to elevate your partner's anxiety.

The What Works List

When making a list of things you can do to help your partner with anxiety, it is essential to communicate about it effectively. Be specific, question your partner how does it make him feel when you perform specific tasks. How does it feel when you join in breathing exercises? Depending on the personality and level of anxiety, they might even want to be left alone. Maybe they need to be reminded during the panic attack to take short breaths, and then perform this task alone.

Choose the right intervention for particular symptoms. Learn to recognize your partner's needs in time and offer help.

Here is an example of an anxiety relief list:

1. If I am nervously pacing the room and I'm unable to relax, offer to go outside for a walk with me, or suggest I should take a walk outside alone

2. If I am complaining about work without any pauses, distract me by choosing a movie we can watch together, or suggesting a book I can read alone.

3. If I'm obsessing over whether I turned off the iron, reassure me I did and remind me that not repeatedly checking is one step closer to recovering from my OCD.

4. During a panic attack, fast and shallow breathing is helping me. Remind me how to perform it and join me in this task.

The What Doesn't Work List

When we love our partner, we feel we will do anything to help him or her. In our efforts to help, we might not realize that what we are doing is more hurtful. We do mean well, but we don't have experience, patience, or knowledge of what is happening with our partner during an anxiety attack. Sometimes even our partner reinforces us to perform tasks that are bad for his anxiety in the long run.

It may look complicated, but both you and your partner need to be honest about behaviors that don't help alleviate anxiety. It will take time and patience to practice to avoid certain actions that bring relief. Here is an example of "what doesn't work" list:

1. I will never again tell my loved one "just get over it."

2. I won't manipulate my partner's feelings to make them stop this behavior.

3. I won't use drugs or alcohol to get over my partner's behaviors.

4. I won't disrespect my partner's phobias and mock them.

5. I won't reinforce my partner's anxiety by accommodating the behavior.

Having the list of what to do and what not to do when anxiety gets triggered will help you and your partner be more in command of your lives. It will stop you from making your partner's anxiety even worse, and it will put both of you on the right track of overcoming the anxiety. Your relationship will become vibrant, more satisfying, and fulfilling. Anxiety cannot be defeated just by taking the steps on the list. They are just things to do to help your partner overcome fear at that point. You will need to take more serious measures to fully overcome anxiety.

A professional therapist will be of great help. It may take some time to find the right therapist for your partner, and it will take some persistence. Therapists may fit one type of personality but not the other. Be sure your partner is paired with a therapist that is right, and that will help. Encourage and support your partner, and in time you will learn how to manage their anxiety and possibly even watch them completely overcome it.

Bibliography

Becker-Phelps, L. (2016). *Insecure in love: How anxious attachment can make you feel jealous, needy, and worried and what you can do about it.* New Harbinger Publications

Daitch, C. (2013). *Anxious in love: How to manage your anxiety, reduce conflict, and reconnect with your partner.* Oakland, CA: New Harbinger.

Giorgetti, D. (2018). PTSD and Relationships: A survival booklet series to love and be loved (PTSD & Relationships)

Thieda, K. N. (2013). *Loving someone with anxiety: Understanding & helping your partner.*